PRESENTATION SKILLS
FOR QUIVERING WRECKS

PRESENTATION SKILLS FOR QUIVERING WRECKS

Bob Etherington

First published in 2006
This facsimile reprint edition (with new cover) published in 2018 by
Marshall Cavendish Business
An imprint of Marshall Cavendish International

A member of the
Times Publishing Group

Other Marshall Cavendish Offices:
Marshall Cavendish Corporation. 99 White Plains Road, Tarrytown NY 10591-
9001, USA • Marshall Cavendish International (Thailand) Co Ltd. 253 Asoke, 12th
Flr, Sukhumvit 21 Road, Klongtoey Nua, Wattana, Bangkok 10110, Thailand •
Marshall Cavendish (Malaysia) Sdn Bhd, Times Subang, Lot 46, Subang Hi-Tech
Industrial Park, Batu Tiga, 40000 Shah Alam, Selangor Darul Ehsan, Malaysia

Marshall Cavendish is a registered trademark of Times Publishing Limited

National Library Board Singapore Cataloguing-in-Publication Data

Name(s): Etherington, Bob.
Title: Presentation skills for quivering wrecks / by Bob Etherington.
Description: Singapore : Marshall Cavendish Business, 2018. |
First published: 2006.
Identifier(s): OCN 1014491488 | ISBN 978-981-4794-70-1 (paperback)
Subject(s): LCSH: Business presentations. | Public speaking.
Classification: DDC 658.452--dc23

Cover design by Lorraine Aw

Printed in Singapore by Fabulous Printers Pte Ltd

Contents

SECTION 1

There are always three speeches, for every one you actually gave. The one you prepared, the one you gave, and the one you wish you gave.

DALE CARNEGIE

Introduction

"Testing … testing 1 … 2 …3 … [*bomp! bomp!*] is this working? … great …. ah! … yes. … Good-day reader … can you hear me OK? … Great … yes … I am going to talk to you today about the subject of business presentation … stand-up "public speaking" in other words … at conferences, conventions, meetings of various sizes, training workshops, and all that sort of thing.

I have done a lot of research in libraries, bookstores and on the Internet about this and nearly every other public speaking website, book, and course quotes the American version of the *Book of lists* on the subject. In that book it apparently lists public speaking as being the number one human Fear. … Well I've looked and looked through the current UK version of the same book and have to say that I am not able to find that statistic. It may have been there once but it's not there now. So everything is fine then!

There is nothing to worry about … you can put this book back on the shelf and go and get your plane, or the rest of your shopping or whatever else you were planning. Presentations to colleagues, staff, customers, and business partners have turned the corner. Business speakers are now fearless. They have, at last, discovered the secret of good, stand-up, communication. Their visual aids are clear and memorable. With their words they inspire, sell, motivate, and ..." [*OK, that's quite enough of that—Editor*]

Actually the truth about 95% of business presentations, all over the world, is that they are still very bad. And my own research shows, conclusively, that the following truths hold good for them:

1. Most audiences have a single objective: to get out of the room.
2. Most presenters have a single objective: to get off the platform.

The presenters dread them so much that they generally try and forget about them until the very last moment when the inevitable hits them. I was once on an plane at London Heathrow, about to depart with some colleagues to Athens for a major European sales conference. One of the other senior people and (reluctant) conference speakers was sitting across the aisle from me. He had a pad of paper on his knee. "That your presentation, Jim? How's it looking?" I asked. "Oh yes," he replied (nervous laugh) "But I haven't finished it yet ... I'll be fine!" By the time we had taxied to the start of the runway ready for take-off, I noticed that after the words, "Good morning everybody," at the top of the blank sheet, he had written the following: "It's been a busy year ..."

Three hours or so later, as we touched down in Athens, I looked again. The pad was still on his lap. The presentation had not advanced beyond, "It's been a busy year ...." His presentation the next day was a predictable, dreadful mess. But then so were the majority of the others.

I have discovered that most speakers, like my colleague Jim, try to forget the whole thing until the day before. The speaker, by then in a state of suppressed panic, not to mention blind terror, locates his slides on the laptop. He breezes through them, mumbling as he goes, the words he imagines he will say tomorrow. Somehow a vision of himself as Churchill forms in his mind; as if, during the night, he will be transformed into a brilliant orator. This mumbled read-through rehearsal, often only half completed, is usually abandoned as this vision becomes fully formed. This results in the usual, confident: "Ah stuff it … I'll run through it again in the morning" and that's it.

Then comes the night.

As morning breaks, however, the metamorphosis into the fully formed quivering wreck is complete!

It will be all right on the night

The famous, often-articulated, words of countless exasperated directors of under-rehearsed, amateur theatrical performances are just those: "It will be all right on the night!" Except it never, never is. And, most corporate presenters behave in just such an amateur fashion with predictable results.

Yes, business people everywhere still dread their amateurish presentations. Subsequently the events that warrant them are usually a scandalous waste of time, money, and opportunity. Presentations are potentially very useful and extremely persuasive communication tools. But, when dabbled in by the untrained or untalented, they are generally devised and delivered appallingly badly. Despite all that, nobody, anywhere is doing much about it!

This is where **I** come in.

I am going to work with you and show you how to become a good presenter. Notice I didn't say a "brilliant" or "terrific" or "wonderful" presenter. Just becoming a "good" presenter is enough to change your business life in unimaginable ways.

So what? ... Why should I? ...

I'll tell you.

You are going to be shown a set of simple skills with which you can easily:

- become too valuable to keep in your present job at your present pay
- become the envy of your friends and colleagues
- be regularly invited to travel to exotic destinations in at least Business if not First Class
- frequently hear the sound of genuine applause from audiences who wish they could have heard more from you
- be singled out to assist influential people to deliver important messages
- be offered better pay terms and conditions to stay if you threaten to resign
- really annoy your competitors when you are speaking to potential customer audiences at the same event as they are
- enjoy yourself generally and not have to work too hard.

Good presenters are so rare that all those things *can easily* come your way *if* you do what I am about to show you. I didn't use superlatives like *brilliant* or *wonderful* to describe the level you need to aspire to. *Good* is quite enough, simply because 95% of business presenters are generally so bad.

Say to most people: "I'd like you to do a presentation at the big meeting next week" and you will generate in their stomach the biggest fear-knot imaginable. Their legs will tremble … their hearts will palpitate … their palms will go clammy … their voice will tremble … their confidence and sense of well being will collapse … they will become a total quivering wreck! If that's you too, it is quite normal. I can do a lot to eliminate much of your fear and in fact, the solution is so simple that you will find yourself saying: "If I'd known it was that easy I'd have done it years ago."

There are other things too, like presentation construction, audience analysis, body language, voice-tone, delivery, using notes, visual aids, handling questions, generating applause, dealing with difficult people, rehearsal and stage craft—they are all dealt with in this book. All these elements will quickly become as natural to you as they became to some of the great speakers of the 20th century like President John Kennedy, Martin Luther King, Nikita Kruschev, and Sir Winston Churchill. They all used the methods and techniques I am going to show you in these pages. Likewise in the 21st century, if you look around you, you will agree that the world's most successful people are turning out to be the good communicators—and you will soon be one of them.

Give people the impression you work harder than you do

Imagine for a moment what it would feel like to deliver a good presentation. Everyone else on the morning's agenda has done the usual: "Good morning everyone … today I'm going to talk about … drone … drone … [*Yawn … yawn when can we get out of here?—25 tedious minutes pass—then, mercifully*] … well I guess that's it … so … unless any of you have any … er? … well then … No? ... er no? … OK, I guess it's time for a break. Thanks … yes."

Then suddenly … and immediately after lunch, in the "graveyard slot," when everyone in the audience is either exhausted by the terribleness of the morning or drugged by the lunchtime carbohydrates … there's … YOU!

Original … animated … memorable … audible … clear visual aids … provocative opening … concise "call-to-action" summing up … excellent "Q & A," unexpectedly powerful conclusion. And to top it all what do we hear? Applause? Is that Applause? But nobody ever applauds our internal presentations! [*Little did they know you actually engineered* that *with your rhetoric too—more later!*]

Don't you think the feeling you would experience would be unimaginable? A rare, unforgettable moment, in which everything appears to be going just right for you. Sure, it's a lot to ask and it probably won't happen every single time but as a recognized and upcoming "good" presenter, your work life will change dramatically for the better and for only a marginal amount of extra effort! Guaranteed!

How do I know this? Because it happened to me. And because, as the lifestyle gurus say: "Success leaves clues." I'm going to show you what I did (and still do) that takes me all over the world as a business presenter and for a lot of money and job satisfaction. I'm going to give you a lot more than "clues" too; I am going to show you exactly what to do to have a terrific life as a business presenter.

It doesn't matter that your day-to-day professional specialty is accounts, admin, dentistry, sales, engineering, train driving, model-making, procurement, sailing, or oil exploration, or anything. The same techniques apply. I don't care if you say to me, having read the book: "That's all very well but it's different in my organization; we have a set way of doing presentations." Well I have to reply that you wouldn't be reading this book if you didn't think you had a presentation problem to solve.

I used to work for just such a large international company which felt it had to lay down a certain way for executives to conduct presentations. Every year they held a large international management conference. Each year it was in a different capital city. We presenters, "the usual suspects" every year, were all thoroughly schooled in what was wanted. My boss in particular would always take me to one side a month beforehand for a stiff talking to. "OK, we all know you can present well. But this time none of your usual stuff! OK? ... Just give them the facts. Tell them what's going on; that's all. No jokes. No "funnies." No clever-ass visuals. Stick to the company slide format. Am I making myself clear? ... Am I? ... And show me the bullet slides you're going to use and your full script in a couple of weeks before we go!"

So every year I would go away and prepare that presentation: Presentation "A" ... it was the presentation I was NOT going to deliver on the day. It was simply a decoy to keep him off my back. At the same time I would, in parallel, prepare Presentation "B" ... the one I was really going to deliver. It was not seen by the boss beforehand. It was a properly thought out and rehearsed communication vehicle.

It obeyed all the rules of professional rhetoric (which you will learn in this short volume). It hardly met the company format in any respect ... well, maybe the corporate logo on the opening title slide but that was it!

Every single time, when we got to the annual event this is what happened. I was always put on the agenda either last thing before lunch or immediately after lunch. As a well-known "good" presenter I had developed a "reputation" and no other speaker on the day ever wanted to follow directly after me. As I said before I wasn't a "great" presenter, I was (and am) simply "good" and that was threatening enough for the others. Before me, there had always been the usual horrific list of unmemorable cloned presentations—bullet points, raw clip art, monotones, mumbling—pure "Death by Powerpoint." The 350-strong senior management global audience were already bored stiff and dying for the evening to come when they could have a bit of fun and socializing. Nobody could deny the awful, costly reality of it all. (By the way, 10 years ago in the mid 1990s, we used to budget an average $5000 per head total cost for this annual jamboree; that worked out at $1.75m—about 1 million pounds—per event. God knows what similar events are going on, right now, as you read this book and how much they are costing in today's money!). Every single time, about 15 minutes before I was due to go on, my boss would take me to one side again and whisper: "This isn't going well. We might as well not have bothered with the speeches ... just throw a big pile of beer cans into the middle of the room and let them all stand around and chat for three days ... that's all they want. ... They're all falling asleep, I don't know why we do these plenary sessions. The MD's furious! I hope you've got some-thing up your sleeve to wake them all up!

I certainly did ... this year's Presentation "B"—pretty well guaranteed to generate a standing ovation every time. Was I great? ... No, just "good." And just being "good" was always more than enough. The trouble was, the next year it had always been forgotten and I received my usual threats and instructions a month before and I was forced to repeat the "A-B" ritual. My co-presenter colleagues towed the line and did their "same old, same old." I didn't. Ever.

So, despite all the warnings and repeated stiff talking to(s), I got to ride on Concorde a lot, traveled First Class with the MD to assist with presentations in the US, Asia, and Europe. Was pleaded with to extend a three-year work assignment in New York for another two years. Was paid special bonuses to keep me happy. Drove a company Jaguar. Enjoyed company paid-for holidays in South Africa, Hawaii, Singapore, Tokyo, and Hong Kong. Got shares in the company before it went "public." And all that sort of stuff and had a really good time. Tough eh? You can do it too ... just dare to change a little bit.

"But I'm a company man/woman! You're preaching anarchy! ... It may have been OK for you but not everybody can do as he/she pleases! I'm putting this book back right now ..." [*just hold on a minute...please*].

I am sure your department or company has to persuade other people to get onboard various projects you're involved with. These target audiences may be either internal or external people. Let's say you're involved with selling ideas, products or services at some time during the business year. In fact, 98% of corporate executives have to sell such things at some time in order to make progress. How many individuals do you have to talk to, to get a single idea through? How many individual managers do you have to convince to get a project enthusiastically supported and implemented by all? How many prospective customers do you have to talk to get a single new contract? The answer is *lots of them*.

Take that last one ... how many prospective customers do you have to see to get one new deal agreed? As a rough "rule of thumb" let us say you currently have to pursue four, in order to "close" one. Suppose I could show you a way to improve that ratio, and that for every four potential customers you pursued, you could successfully close on two from now on. How would that go down in your organization? A 100% improvement—all achieved in a lot less time. The way you can do it is to put on a rehearsed and well-delivered, *good presentation*.

It is exactly the way we do the primary marketing for our own London-based training business. We advertise an "open" presentation during which we present what we can do to help people and companies achieve their own business goals. There is often a waiting list for these presentations. Some people come back for a second boost every couple of years. And what's more, these quarterly events are not free. Delegates happily pay about over £100 (US$150 plus) per seat to attend a three-hour seminar. Their individual objectives are clearly to obtain some up-to-date techniques to help them sell their own products and services. Their desires are met because we make sure that they get these in abundance during the three hours. Meanwhile the corporate objective for our company in delivering these presentations, is to sell the audience what more we can do, on a tailored basis, for individual organizations.

Every time we give one of these open presentations we can guarantee to convert far more prospective clients into full long term clients—and in a very short space of time, shorter than any other way I can think of.

Once you put on a presentation you are setting yourself apart from your competitors. They always go the easy way … not because they're stupid but because they're lazy. They carry on with the one-on-one phone calls, face-to-face persuading, emails, and hard-copy letters. By presenting "live" to a large group you differentiate your own offering from all your competitors and generate a feeling of professional competence in the audience. Good presenters are treated with awe.

Save time! (Actually you can't. You can only spend it)

Another great thing about putting on a good presentation is the time it saves! I don't know about you but I have a good few other things I'd like to be doing with my time everyday rather than chasing business opportunities. When I have the chance to sell my business services to a large complex account there always seem to be at least four people involved with the decision. I've even developed a little formula to tell me whether the time I will probably spend on it will make winning the business worth the effort. But one great time-cutter is finding an excuse to invite all the decision makers to a single presentation.

If you see all the decision makers individually, you will most often find that they call you a few days later with more questions. Answering these often means another trip to see the person in order to resolve the further queries. Another great chunk of unsavable time used up. On the other hand when they are all in the room together for your presentation, the psychological dynamics of the group often results in all the necessary questions coming out together. Everybody learns the concerns and needs of the other decision makers. And very often, during the "Q&A," you will find you hear very little argument and the people who are already on your side will strongly support your proposition.

> *Tip*: If you ask for and are granted permission to deliver a presentation and this gives your customer the idea to get some of your competitors in too, make sure you secure the last slot on the day. A good presentation is not only rare but it makes the whole of your project a big-deal and if you want them to remember you particularly well, go on last. On Broadway they always have the hit tune toward the end of the show—as they say: "Leave them singing your song."

It is often the case that a company or department that believes it has a superior product or idea, loses out, in a competitive environment, not because they actually have a poor product but because they are outsold by the other side. The fact is we humans tend to make most of our "buying" decisions based on emotional drivers, which are then justified in the human brain with facts. Extremely intelligent, well-educated people argue this point with me for hours and tell me point blank that they are much too wise and sophisticated to be bamboozled with a presentation behind which there is very little substance; they just want the facts. Well here's a "fact" for you: all the current research confirms that business audiences start losing concentration in a "facts only" presentation within about 30 seconds of the start! This is not about bamboozling, it is about using the way the audience brain works—every audience brain.

A good presenter knows that the contagion of enthusiasm is transmitted by a lot more than the facts alone. If you are ever surprised that you have lost a deal and then told it was "because of the price," be suspicious. Be very suspicious. "Too expensive" is the easy objection. More often than not, it was because the way you presented your proposition was perceived as boring, samey, sloppy, disorganized, unrehearsed, monotone, and did not address the thinking of this audience. A good presenter always anticipates that every person in the audience is asking the one huge, unspoken question: "What's in this for me?" And as a good presenter you need to answer that question. If you don't, it will affect the perceived quality of your delivery because (like it or not) it will be seen as a precise reflection of the professionalism of your organization or department.

One of my clients, a senior director in a large European oil company, told me that he despairs of getting some of his very bright geologists to understand this. He asks how these PhDs and BSc educated people can expect to win international business when they turn up to present their ideas to potential customers dressed in a sweater, jeans, and Doc Martin boots. Then try to deliver their message by reading off Powerpoint slides with their hands in their pockets. It is NOT just your facts it's the way you deliver them that makes the winning difference.

Most quivering wrecks still don't know that a man called Professor Albert Mehrabian carried out some investigative research several years ago, to find out which factors most influence an audience during a presentation. The results were startling. They showed that most of what an audience remembers are things they have seen. The next important factor is the tone of voice used by the presenter and least influential factor is the actual content of the presentation.

The ratios are:

- Visual impact 55%
- Tone of voice 38%
- Text and Content 7%

It's not that the content isn't important, of course it is. But if you fail to get the visual side of it (body language and

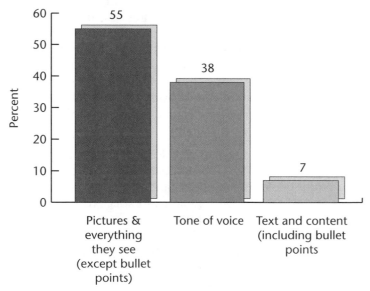

The way audiences remember presentation content

pictures) right and then compound that failure by not sounding right, then the content doesn't matter at all.

One final point before we burst into the book. About three or four times a week our training business is presented with CVs from aspiring trainers who would like to get on the team. When I call them they all tell me they are great trainers. But when I ask them about their presentation skills, particularly stand up presentations to potential clients, they go quiet. One said to me a few weeks ago: "Mr Etherington I don't think you heard me. I'm a trainer not a presenter!" That's when the application—as with all other similar conversations—gets summarily terminated. There is no shortage of trainers in my market, just like there's no shortage of "product" in most markets. The great, global shortage is of people who can successfully communicate and present ideas. Yet most companies are doing very little to rectify the problem.

It's as simple as this: If you or your company keep doing your presentations the same way that you've always done them, the same problems will recur. As the saying goes:

> If you always do what you've always done,
> You'll always get what you've always got.

Still with me?

You may have got this far into the introduction and be saying to yourself something along the lines of: "This book is no good for me at all! I **am** a quivering wreck! No don't laugh … I **really** am a quivering wreck! I am a heaving ball of jelly when it comes to standing up in front of an audience. That's me. Awful. Can't do it. Will never be able to. I'm awful. Nobody's as awful as me."

So allow me to relate a story I heard 20 years ago in a radio broadcast about Parliament and the House of Commons in

London. The speaker was a successful middle-aged man who was recalling his very early days as a Member of Parliament. The particular topic of the program was the first occasion, as a young man, on which he was due to make a speech on the floor of the House; his so-called maiden speech.

The tradition is, for a maiden speech in the House of Commons, that the Member of Parliament is not allowed to read it! He or she has to deliver it cold. The young MP was sure he had all his facts in order but was a total bag of nerves. He had only five minutes to speak in the particular debate but could neither eat nor sleep for days before. He was losing weight. He could think of nothing else. He imagined over and over again failing disastrously. He imagined the laughter and hoots of derision when he messed up. He would mess up. He knew he would mess up.

On the day he sat nervously in his place next to an old hand who had been an MP for years. When he was finally called to speak he prepared to stand and as he did so felt a restraining hand on his arm; it was the old hand. "Enjoy yourself son," the kindly voice whispered into the maiden speaker's ear, "Nobody's expecting much!"

"Nobody's expecting much" should be your mantra too. If it's true, and it is, that all business audiences are expecting the usual rubbish, you have nothing to be petrified about. You are either going to meet their expectations by being awful or surprise them (if you apply what's in this book) by being good. It is a simple choice. You are choosing, from now on to be a "good" presenter and enjoy the huge rewards it will bring you.

SECTION 2

When the imagination and will power are in conflict, are antagonistic, it is always the imagination which wins, without any exception.

EMIL COUÉ – 19TH CENTURY PSYCHOLOGIST

The art of "don't worry" for the quivering wreck

I was a copying machine salesman in the early 1970s. I had been an engineer but it bored me. I wanted glamor, a company car, an expense account, and an easy life on the road. Actually it was tough. My first sales territory was about one square mile of dilapidated South London. My various managers would often tell me on tough days: "Don't worry, be happy!" or "Don't be so negative! Think positive." When I heard these great motivational mantras I had an overwhelming desire to thump them. "What?" I always thought, "'Be positive?' I've earned this depression and I'm damn well going to have it!"

First of all telling somebody *not* to do something ("Ah! … don't worry about the presentation so much!") as a way of getting them to stop doing something is a complete waste of time because neither your brain nor mine can hold a negative thought. Motivational speakers regularly illustrate this point by telling a corporate audience: "Don't think of pink giraffes" (It's the example they *all* use for some reason) Then they say: "What are you all thinking about?" and the reply comes back, "Pink giraffes! Ha … ha … ha!"

A common example of this phenomenon is when parents see their daughter, between about four to eight years of age, dressed in her best new party dress at a family party. The child has "grown up" enough to go up to the table where the drinks are and get a glass of orange juice. The filled glass is lifted carefully down from the table and is being carefully carried back to their seat. Everything is going well so far— great concentration; tongue out to make sure nothing goes wrong; taking careful steps; no rushing; it is all going swimmingly well so far; no accidents; no sign of an upcoming problem. Then comes the mistake ... not committed by the child ... but by the adult! "Don't spill it!"

Now, I told you earlier that the human brain can't hold a negative thought. The child's brain doesn't hold on to the *Don't...* it only hears the **spill it!**. So what do you think the child, who is dressed in her best dress, associates with accidental spillage (which incidentally hadn't even been on their mental menu up to this point)? Yes you've got it—parental anger and trouble of all sorts too terrible to envisage. The anticipation of this terrible event generates a little picture of upcoming fearful consequences ... and when we're afraid we tremble, we quiver and what do you think happens to the orange juice when the quivering begins? Correct: spillage!

Telling someone, anyone (even yourself) *not* to do something is a great way of reinforcing the very bad behavior you're trying to avoid. So if you ever indulge in a little bit of talking to yourself to bolster courage for your next presentation ("Come on **me** pull yourself together! You don't want to make a fool of yourself!") you are setting yourself up for a disaster. So let us make sure in future it is a conversation that has the desired effect!

"Every day in every way I am getting better and better!"... I am really ... I think ... or am I?!

At the beginning of the 20th century a French pharmacist called Émile Coué started the whole positive thinking thing going. He introduced a method of psychotherapy based on a regular daily affirmation. Followers of his method were required, at regular times during the day, to repeat to themselves: "Every day in every way I am getting better and better." This constant repetition was supposed to engender in the subject an increasing feeling of confidence and self-esteem. It certainly worked for quite a few people but the reason it worked so well for them, yet hardly had any effect on others, wasn't understood for several more years.

It was half a century later that they discovered that the people for whom the method worked well could immediately imagine themselves getting better and better. The process of imagining was doing a lot more than the words themselves. In fact, the more vividly the person could imagine the improvement and could imagine what they would be doing and how they would be acting when the improvement came about, the better it worked.

In addition, the more senses the person could use, to experience this *imagined future*, the better it worked. The dominant sense was always sight, followed by sound, followed by smell. Now although I use this method myself I, personally, cannot imagine the "smell" of success but if you can, it looks like you're going to do even better with this than me. I can *see* with my, so-called mind's eye (some days better than others) and I can *hear* voices, sounds, applause etc. in my imagination. I can even *feel* an imagined touch but smell it? ... No. However this method really works, even if you are only able to implement it in a less than perfect way. So now I am going to show you how to do it too.

This is beyond simple "positive thinking"

Instead of focusing on what you don't want to happen "*I don't want to make a mess of this,*" you need to make your self-talk a lot more positive. So even if you don't believe it yet, I want you to say these words: "I am going to be really great at this next presentation." (But here's the powerful part), you now need to shut your eyes and imagine yourself on the platform in front of the audience and see, in your mind's-eye everybody cheering and feel yourself being very pleased.

Hang on … hang on just a minute … I already know it … you're saying "What a load of rubbish!" and beginning to skip this bit—but will you join me in a quick experiment *please… please?* I want to prove to you right now how powerful this self-talk combined with visualization really is.

Brain proof exercise for skeptics

I use this little instant-proof, live-demonstration-in-your-own-home, example in just about all my training seminars and if you've attended a course of mine or read any of my other written material you'll probably know it already but bear with me. OK, stand up and if you're right handed raise your right arm straight out in front of you with your index finger extended pointing like a sign-post straight ahead. If you're left handed do the same with your left arm and hand. Now, right handed person, keeping your feet firmly planted on the floor and your arm out-stretched swing your torso to the right and see how far round you can twist and note an object you can point to that shows how far round you got. Then come back. Left-handed people do the same but you swing round to the left. Then come back to the starting point.

Now stay standing and shut your eyes. I want you now to imagine (don't move at all) just imagine, in your mind's-eye, swinging around again. But this time, in your imagination, reach the same object you stopped at last time but find your self able to twist further round this "imagined" time ... much further ... 4in ... 8in ... 12in ... 16in ... effortlessly. Note how far you imagined you got to this time. Then in your mind's-eye come back to your starting point and open your eyes.

Now, arm up, finger pointing do it again. Really swing your body round again this time ... and what happened? How far did you manage to swing this time? Were you surprised to find that, along with over 80% of people who do this, the second time you *really* did it, you could, effortlessly, swing much further than the first time?

But nothing physical has changed. You didn't suddenly develop the qualities of a circus contortionist or top gymnast. All you did was put a different picture in your head. You put that picture there, just once, half a minute ago. You didn't believe it necessarily but your brain was completely fooled by the picture you chose, into believing that you could ... so you did.

You see, the human brain is startlingly naïve. It does not know the difference between real and imagined events! If you tell it something is so and it is a physical possibility that it could be so, it sets about getting you to do it. By the way, you cannot break the laws of physics and for example, fly by flapping your arms, or breathe underwater, or levitate or any other daft stuff so "don't even go there."

Yes, if you say so: you're a quivering wreck

If you tell your brain over and over that, when it comes to business presenting you're a quivering wreck and you can imagine (pictures in your head) failing disastrously next time, your brain will unfailingly give you the result you want. You are what you tell yourself you are and, amazingly, other people accept you for the value you appear to be placing on yourself.

Yes, if you say so: you're a fearless presenter

Now … knowing the little you have already proved to yourself, it is time to give you a very practical set of instructions to make you think like a good presenter. These instructions are based on modern sports psychology. I often hear top-of-their-game professional golfers and tennis players talk about their need to see, in their mind's-eye, the ball going into the hole or over the net before the game.

Similarly in the world of business—the PhD who taught me to negotiate, had studied for years the part played by experience and training in becoming a top negotiator—but in the end had concluded that the negotiators who succeeded most often were those who had clearly imagined each success beforehand.

Believe it or not, this imaginary picturing is deadly serious stuff.

Learn to visualize being a brilliant presenter

The thought process which is concerned with seeing yourself in your mind's-eye performing at your optimum level is known as visualization (what a surprise!). The most important aspect of this is "mental practice." Mental practice involves going over and over in your head some important event and combining it with as many senses as you can, especially mental imagery. Professional sports people of all types use it to keep their minds focused on critical competitions, tournaments, and potential record breaking opportunities, and away from inner tension, rivalries, possible failure, and accidents. It works just as well in any area of your life when you want to raise yourself up to your maximum potential.

Professional mental practice techniques can be internally or externally focused. When you focus externally you imagine being in an audience watching yourself perform. When you focus internally, as described previously, you place yourself in the imagined event and become the performer rather than the audience. When you start practicing this technique you can chose either focus method. What follows is a guide for those who want to do it externally. So you will be in the audience.

Professional mental practice can build a total feeling of invincibility, change your attitude and boost your confidence.

External mental practice

The best and probably the most effective mental practice technique is called "top performance mental practice." To start with, sports people compile a list of the attributes they associate with top performance in their own particular field. Top performance for a professional golfer, for instance, would probably include perfect swing, accurate putting, terrific concentration as well as total mental focus, self-confident attitude and a feeling of being totally ready to play.

For you, the upcoming effective presenter, it would doubtless include upright and confident body language, a sincere authoritative and powerful voice, a terrific mastery of your subject, a self-confident attitude and feeling of being totally "rehearsed" and ready to go.

Now you need to compose a very detailed imaginary picture in your head. Think back to a moment in your own history when you actually, despite all your prior misgivings, did well at a presentation or meeting. If you really (really) can't recall such an occasion make it up ... invent how you think such a presentation would have been! I repeat the point I made earlier in this book: *your subconscious mind does not know the difference between real and imagined events.* So go ahead ... imagine something terrific! The visualization process requires reflecting on this real or imagined top performance, particularly the characteristics and behaviors which make it your best performance.

Detailed instructions

Step 1: **You need to relax**. Get yourself into a comfortable position either lying down or sitting in an easy chair. Breathe in deeply and slowly over three seconds, breathe out over three seconds. Keep doing this for one minute until you're relaxed. (*Now don't give up already!! Just before the 2004 Olympics in Athens, I watched, on TV, a Russian gymnastic coach get a young aspiring female athlete to go through this* precise set of instructions, *in order to perform, 30 minutes later, a qualifying routine she had been failing at!*)

Step 2: **You need to visualize**. In your mind's-eye, imagine you are in front of a large cinema screen. On to the screen I want you to project a film of yourself standing in front of a business audience delivering a brilliant presentation. You're actually in the audience watching a clone of yourself perform; an out-of-body experience! Now think, as you watch "you" perform, just how did you feel before you stood up to deliver this brilliant oration? What self-talk was going on in your head? Remember, if you can, the feeling of confidence—real or imagined—that you had.

See yourself as clearly as you can in this upright, confident, and strong state. Focus as much as you can on every aspect of your being: the look of you, what you were feeling, the smells, what you could see, how you had decided to stand, how your heart was beating, your facial expression ... everything that contributed to your top performance. Feel these sensations becoming branded on your mind so that you can bring them back whenever you want to. By doing this you will be able to describe all the things that have in the past contributed to a feeling of "King of the world" confidence.

Now make the screen blank, and let another scene appear on the screen. The movie is no longer historical. You are now projecting forward to an upcoming speaking event—one which hasn't happened yet. You are going to be a key speaker at this future event. Once again tap in to those same feelings and sensations you recalled from the real or imagined event from your past. The one in which you performed perfectly, strongly, confidently! Know for sure that everything will once again work wonderfully for you in the future event as it did in the past. You feel confident, in control, a complete dominant personality.

As you continue to watch the future movie see yourself up there on the platform in a state of complete concentration. You're alert, totally in the present. This state you can see is giving you everything you want: audience reaction ... smooth delivery ... commanding voice ... genuine laughter ... applause. Identify each vital outcome that you desire from your presentation. See each of those outcomes actually happening in your imagination. See each of your own desirable characteristics actually happening in front of you.

Step 3: **You need to reinforce regularly**. We human beings learn by doing things over and over again. So repeat this mental exercise at least once every day. I do mine first thing in the morning and last thing at night. (*What, you still do it!?*) Of course. You see, the secrets to success are all around us all the time. It's just that 95% of the human race is too lazy to spot them or do anything about them.

Success leaves clues. So I copy what other very successful people do. They practice over and over again. It's in all the books and autobiographies they write. Sportsmen and women especially—they mentally rehearse constantly. When they get lazy about it they find they start to lose. In some recent academic research into what makes lucky business people "lucky" it was revealed that nearly all of them admit to setting some time aside every day just to imagine, think, contemplate or meditate. So I do too. I imagine myself regularly, sharply, clearly, where I want to be. And it certainly works ... even when I think it's not working! I don't understand it, I just do it because it works even when my visualization is not as clear as I would like it to be on some days.

> "If I don't practice for one day, I know it. If I don't practice for two days the critics know it. If I don't practice for three days the audience know it"
> PADEREWSKI THE FAMOUS RUSSIAN CONCERT PIANIST

Internal mental practice

The second technique of mental practice is internally focused. Instead of watching yourself on a movie screen, this time get inside your own head. Look out of your eyes. Hear with your own ears. Let your own hands feel the wooden edge of the imaginary podium or table. You are the performer looking out over the imaginary audience. Feel the carpet beneath your feet. Hear the applause for you. See the senior people or clients looking up to you and nodding in agreement. Feel yourself looking straight back at them and holding their gaze. Feel yourself smiling. Hear an imagined question from an audience member and hear your clear, measured answer.

Some presenters I know who often have to speak to relatively cynical or even potentially cynical audiences (for me these are often company sales conventions) take this whole idea one stage further and imagine the audience as if they were stark naked or wearing paper party hats and so on. Another associate of mine is a very relaxed Richard Branson style of dresser. He is quite intimidated by an audience in formal business attire: dark suit and tie. So he imagines them in faded, scruffy, worn jeans. You can do that too or maybe make them very thin or hugely fat. Or see them all as kids in highchairs. My personal favorite is to see them all with long trunks, sticking-out ears and "false moustache and glasses" sets. You can visualize them anyway you like.

The thing you will find is that once you have placed them in this context it is never possible to feel the same way about them again. Fear is a total imaginary imposter itself. Remember that fear itself is spelt F.E.A.R. and stands for **F**ictitious **E**vents **A**ppearing **R**eal. Try it if you don't believe me. Try to feel exactly the same about talking to ludicrous people with trunks and big ears as you would about fearsome dark suited business executives. You just can't.

As with any new skill it will take you a while to practice and get comfortable doing all these things. It won't always go beautifully when you HAVE practiced for a while. But persistence, easily the most important factor in this, will pay off for you. A few years ago, at the age of 44, I learned to fly. Each lesson was, unbeknown to my instructor, going to be my last. I was that petrified; yes a total quivering wreck! Yet even though I couldn't feel it working I still did my regular visualizing. I always said to myself, very negatively and against ALL my principles: "One more lesson … then I'll tell him it's not for me." Yet each week I found I was doing more and more of the flying without instruction. Then I started to rationalize it … "OK I can fly straight and level now, but turning, that's another matter" … then a couple of weeks later: "OK I can fly straight, turn, climb, descend, but I'll never be able to learn to talk on the radio! And as for learning Morse code, recovering from spiral dives and stalls, and navigation, not to mention my 'first solo' … FORGET it." And so it went on *but I persisted with the internal mental practice.* I constantly imagined myself as a brilliant Red Arrows style pilot. In my mind I was looking out of the window, talking on the radio. Recovering from stalls like a natural. Four weeks later I flew my first solo. Four months later I got my license. Now I can't stop flying! Don't give up on the mental practice!

Summary

The principle goal of mental practice is to give you high-level, consistent performance in whatever area you have chosen. You must practice the technique at least once every day for 30 days initially and if you're serious (*you ARE serious aren't you?*) should get started in the next 72 hours. Psychologists tell us that with any new project if we don't move from thought to action in the next three days, then it is 80% likely that we will never start.

When choosing whether to use internal mental practice or external mental practice I recommend you alternate each day. But do it each day. It really doesn't matter whether you think it is working or not, it works for everyone who does it. Don't discuss it with highly intellectual people or close friends who, I have found will often dismiss it on the basis that, "if it was that easy everybody would do it." Well "everybody" doesn't do it but the few who do (like me) find that mental practice works every time.

This is very powerful stuff for quivering wrecks with a deep desire to transform themselves. If you're still on the fence and not sure whether you can be bothered with it take the following quick check right now:

1. Write down all the benefits of NOT taking this action.
2. Write down all the benefits of taking the action.
3. Write down the COSTS of not acting.*
4. Write down the COSTS of acting.
5. Keep going. Don't stop until the benefits of taking action outweigh the benefits for NOT taking action by 10 to 100 times and the costs for NOT taking action outweigh the costs for taking action by 10 to 100 times

The growing psychological science built on mental practice and visualizing is called Neuro Linguistic Programming or "NLP." For the past 15 years there have been a growing number of books and courses available for those who desire to study and apply the methods in more depth. You can do an Internet search on "NLP" and you will find pages of hits. This book, on the other hand, is specifically about presentation skills so we won't be going into much more depth on the subject. Suffice it to say you can use the little we have discussed here to rapidly transform you outlook from quivering wreck to requested orator.

So now forward to what we need to discuss: the actual compilation and delivery of a brilliant presentation. For that simply turn the page.

---

*For step 3, you can consider the costs of not doing this mental rehearsal in these areas:

spiritual, social, intellectual, financial, physical, emotional.

SECTION 3

If you're not practicing, somebody else is, somewhere,
and he'll be ready to take your job.

BROOKS ROBINSON – AMERICAN PROFESSIONAL
BASEBALL PLAYER

Prior preparation prevents pathetically poor performance

We had to get some of the personal psychology sorted out in Chapter 1, because it is so very important. After all, this book is about "Presentation skills for Quivering Wrecks" so concentrating on the "QW" part first is probably a good idea. But now we have to move on and get on with the first lesson—which is concerned with the actual thing called "a presentation."

First of all I have to tell you what it is not. It is a harsh lesson and one has to be cruel to be kind. There is no way I can break this to you gently. I have thought and thought but arrived at the conclusion that I just have to come right out with it. So here goes … **"Presentation skills 101:"**

Your slide show is NOT your presentation; YOU are your presentation.

There I've said it!

I know this is not what the makers of data-projectors and slide-software packages are telling you but it is the unvarnished, naked truth.

A few years ago a British husband and wife team (he: songwriter, she: singer) whose main claim to fame was writing and singing jingles and theme tunes for soap operas and TV ads, put on a one week show at the London Palladium. It was just them … nobody else for nearly three hours. The first-night critic gave this verdict: "The one good thing that can be said of their show is that they did finally stop!" That is how most of us view the average slide-show presentation. "When Lord, oh when, is it going to end?"

I have no ax to grind and no hardware or software to sell you, so I want to remind you of why this is so. Every one of us these days has exactly the same sophisticated presentation technology on our desktops and laptops no matter where in the world we live. When I watch you present to me, I don't marvel at your ability to fade and dissolve slides or make your "bullets" segue into position from the side, top or bottom. I won't laugh uncontrollably at your team-building bullet: THERE'S NO "I" IN "T.E.A.M." Your clipart doesn't thrill me and I don't think it was you who artistically created those bland little pictures.

In fact, I will probably die of boredom if I ever see that clipart of the triumphal manager walking up to the top of the mountain, carrying a flag, again. Or the picture of a target with an arrow in it. Or the two hands firmly shaking. Or the man in the blue suit with his back to the audience with his arms outstretched and placed in the bottom right hand corner as if he is looking up and embracing the tedious bullet points above him. Or the duck with an ax about to cleave a PC screen in half. Or a Globe with anything on it

I know how you did it because I can do it too! I have the same clipart. I'm not impressed.

In the old days—about 15 years ago—we were still using 35mm glass slides. You had to have somebody else make them up for you. They were very expensive. Not better than today just more expensive! However, from an audience point of view it was a marginally better arrangement. You see, as the audience approached their terminal boredom level halfway through the morning, they still had a straw of hope they could cling to. The slides were usually carried on top of the projector in a circular plastic carousel. Each carousel could hold 50 slides. As the presentation progressed the carousel would turn with a rattling noise and the next slide would audibly click into position as the previous slide was moved on. It was possible back then for an audience member to take a glance at the carousel projector at the back of the room and estimate, from the position of the carousel, the number of slides which hadn't yet been shown. From that it was possible to gauge how much longer they all had to endure the tedium. These days no such luck! Everything is inside the computer and we don't know—we simply can't tell—when it will end.

Audiences (that's sometimes you and me) are sitting there asking one question. Sometimes it is articulated, mostly it is unconscious—the question is, "What's in this for me?" Yet most audiences only hear one thing before falling into the pit of boredom: what's in it for the company, the organization or the presenter. The secret of avoiding these problems and benefiting from each of your appearances is one word: **"Preparation."**

But here's where it all starts to go wrong before you have even begun. Most presenters do not prepare. Most presenters do not prepare. Most presenters do not prepare. But many presenters think they prepare, so let us look at what preparation is not:

- Putting together a few slides the night before
- Borrowing somebody else's slides and mixing them in with a few of your own

- Agreeing to present a complete set of somebody else's slides because you've been told to
- Writing a word-for-word script and hardly looking at it or reading it out loud until "the day."

The above is at the heart of the presentations which bore us all to death.

Preparation and its twin sister **rehearsal** have major benefits for quivering wrecks:

Taken together they eliminate 75% of nerves

So what are the steps toward adequate preparation that will eliminate 75% of your nerves?

There are 8 of them. They are very simple. Taking them can change your life. Most presenters don't bother with them. Those presenters are stark staring mad. Even when they have read this book they won't do anything different. These are the steps:

8. When are you going to rehearse?

7. How will you enthuse?

6. Where are your pictures?

5. How are you going to open?

4. How are you going to close? (Going for the big fizzle)

3. Why that content? (I can't remember what you just said)

2. Who's your audience? (Think of them all as cabbages…..yeah right!)

1. Where's the goal?

Taking the steps

1. What is your point and what's the goal?

I make presentations at many conferences all over the world. Some of these conferences and conventions are two days long or even more. Sometimes I am also the facilitator, compere, narrator, master of ceremonies or conference leader. In other words I'm the man that keeps the pot simmering.

I warm up the audience on the first morning and wake them up after lunch. I tell them what is going to happen and how the agenda will unfold. I "chair" panel discussions on subjects important to a particular company or organization. Often I get a key-note slot of my own and lead a seminar on selling, presenting, negotiating, or simply what it is we do when performing at our peak level.

The requested selling topic is often on the subject: "Telling isn't selling." Most sales people when they are asked to sell something are congenitally programmed to talk and talk and talk ... and talk. They have all been on training courses that show them why this approach is doomed to failure. But in the field, in front of customers, they instantly return to old habits. Facts, facts, facts and stuff, stuff, stuff. They wonder why they don't sell much. They should wonder no longer—there is simply far too much stuff there.

Humans are very bad at absorbing and making sense of loads of stuff in a very short timescale. That's why, these days, we often hear the phrase: "Too much information!" or "Information overload!" The same applies to most business presentations; far too much stuff. To prove to the audience the uselessness of too much "stuff" in any persuasive presentation I ask them to cast their minds back to the previous morning when the conference opened:

"Do you remember at 9am yesterday morning there was an opening presentation?"
[*The audience murmur "Yes"*]

"How long did the opening presentation last?
["*About 30 minutes*"]

"Can anybody give me a 30-second précis of the presentation?"
[*There is usually silence*]

"Can anybody give me the title or general theme?"
[*There is usually silence*]

"Can anbody tell me the name of the presenter?"
[*There is usually silence*]

The cause of the silence is chiefly down to the massive pile of "stuff" that the presenter has packed into his or her 30-minute presentation. The fact that the presentation was almost certainly appallingly badly delivered by the presenter did not help. But all those points, facts, and stuff made the brains of the collective audience freeze, then give up and tune out. That's why they remember nothing; there's nothing there. It's all been dumped.

They just don't get it!

When I first became a trainer, one of the biggest shocks was how little people's brains retain after a few hours lecturing. You're generally lucky if a class recalls one-third or a quarter of what you intended. One further problem is that they all remember a different third or quarter. In their early days in front of a corporate audience, many apprentice trainers and tutors believe that it is all down to the "thick" delegate groups set before them: "This lot are particularly brainless!" It takes a long while for the trainer, presenter or speaker to realize and then admit that the problem lies not with the audience but with the teacher.

Someone, I can't recall who it was, once told me that the British Prime Minister during the late 1950s and early 1960s, Sir Harold MacMillan, had given any young MP in the House of Commons the following advice: "When you've been an MP for between one and ten years your speech should contain no more than one point. When you've been an MP for between ten and twenty years you'll have enough experience to raise it to two points. Anything over twenty years as an MP and you can raise it to three points but that's it! Three points, maximum, is all you'll get across in any speech!"

So now you need to decide the point that you want to get across. (*OK, you can have three if you really—really—want but as a quivering wreck you will be 100% better off if you take my advice and articulate one single point. I promise you will … so what is it to be?*)

If you're stuck here's some guidance

Let's say you are the manager of a bank. The point of your speech should, therefore, *not* be: "The point of my speech is to tell them about my bank." Or if you're a project manager, *not*: "The point of my speech is to let them know about the project." Or if you're a veterinary doctor, *not*: "The point of my speech is to tell them about dogs."

If you set down any of the above as your "point" you are back at square one. The subject you have chosen is far too broad and by implication packed with points—too much "stuff."

Go ahead be selfish—your Point should be about YOU

Your chosen "point" for your presentation should be refined to a razor's edge. Sharpening your point in such a way, will enable you to be more focused in delivery and subsequently memorable. It is the only point in your preparation where you may use the words "I" or "My." "I" and "My" are the commonest, yet least persuasive, words in the business world. But I am giving you permission to use them right now and in this part of the preparation only. You should focus your point on what you personally need to get from this presentation. Is it money? A raise? Support from senior management? The whole salesforce motivated? The audience to understand why redundancies may be necessary?

This concentration on yourself and how you will benefit from doing a half decent job on this upcoming presentation is a significant motivator for you. It will start you on the road to not wanting to make a boring idiot of yourself. It is not something you should just think about either. Once your point is pretty well decided then you need to get it down on paper.

An effective point looks similar to this:

- "The point of my speech is to get the Board to give my team $250,000 to complete the project"
- "The point of my speech is that afterward the audience will recognize why I have to let people go"
- "At the conclusion of my speech I will have demonstrated why the audience should award the business to my company."

So if you're about to prepare for your next presentation, take a sheet of plain white paper and write across the top:

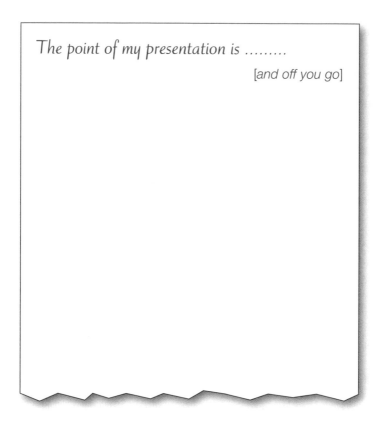

The point of my presentation is ....

[*and off you go*]

Note: If you *have* to have two or even three points you need to get across then go ahead and write them down too. But you will have a much more dynamic and memorable effect if at this stage you fix on one ... *Promise!* ... I'll say no more!

2. Who's your audience? (*Think of them all as cabbages*)

In my very first sales office there was a big poster on the wall. It pictured a scowling, miserable, balding, middle-aged man sitting in a typical boss's chair. Under it was this caption:

> "I don't know who you are
> I don't know what you do
> I don't care about your business
> I don't care why you were delayed
> I don't care whose fault it is
> I don't care about your products
> I don't care about your family
> I don't care about your salary
> I don't care about your promotion
> And I really don't care whether
> you make a profit or not...
>
> Now ... what do you want to sell me?"

It may be cruel and heartless, and you may say what a miserable old git! Yet the truth is that most audiences in most presentations where ideas, products or services are being presented are, at some level of their consciousness, saying something along the lines of those very words to themselves. In essence they are asking: "What's in this for me?" Because, like it or not, most people are chiefly interested in themselves. So when you stand up, your "point," which was very correctly and concisely crafted in the previous step, now needs to be translated into the language of "You."

> "The bad news is a lot of you have been made
> redundant. The good news is ... I've been promoted! .....
> .... Ah ... I can see most of you are still on the
> bad news."
>
> RICKY GERVAIS AS DAVID BRENT IN THE
> BBC TV SERIES "THE OFFICE"

A word about "You"

"You" is the rarest word in business communication. Unlike the most common, yet least persuasive, words that you were introduced to in Step 1 ("I" and "My"), "You" is by far the most persuasive.

When you make your presentation, the whole thing should focus on the professional language, anticipated needs, continuing problems, and motivations of the audience you are addressing. The simplest audiences to plan for are the single strata—all one type. They might be all main board directors of your company, or all accountants, or all engineers. Now, **you** know what point **you** need to get across. But what do most board members want to hear? What professional language do accountants speak? What do engineers understand? To get your point across to any audience you need to spend some time analyzing and finding out about the way they see the world. Here are three sample audiences you may come across in any company. The board of directors, the accountants, and your own team

Board of directors

Board members, for example, want to hear your presentation in terms of "the future." Boards of directors are employed to guide the company down the path to new horizons. The current day-to-day business of the company is managed by middle managers. The board on the other hand sit amid their climate-controlled, upstairs offices, thinking, planning, considering all the options. So when you stand up what are you going to be talking about in terms of your "point"? You want some more budget allocated to your project ... fine! But the board will want to know how that allocation—*if* they give it to you—will address the future needs of the organization two to three years down the road. So that's the story you need to devise around your "point" for the board.

The bean counters

You may also, later that day, have to address the finance team about your budget. The board may want some input from the "bean counters" before agreeing to allocate the funds. It is probably not going to be particularly useful to make the same presentation to them about all that "two-to-three-years-down-the-road" stuff. The accountants' horizons probably extend as far as the end of the current fiscal year. So the story you need to tell them will probably be illustrated in terms of the immediate financial benefits, of allocating the funds you want this year, and the regular reporting system you will be setting up to ensure that spending is controlled on a monthly basis. Same "point" different story.

Your own team

When you talk to your own team about the possible new budget allocation, you may touch upon the future of the organization. You will mention *firmly* the need for all of them to stick to the accurate reporting requirements in order to keep "accounts" happy. But the major story for your team must be the effect on their own careers and their prospects if they achieve the agreed project goals on time and on budget. Same point once again but again a different story.

On each occasion the different audiences will only understand what you want in terms of what they want.

In "selling school" sales people are taught that you can sell precisely the same product to completely different customers by first finding out what they want to buy, then selling only those aspects of the product to that customer and ignoring the others. For example, a rich little old lady might well want to buy a Jaguar car to drive. A bit of probing will probably reveal that she is interested mostly in comfort and safety. The comfy soft leather seats, the internal seat warmers for cold days, the electric seat raiser which gets her up high enough to see over the steering wheel, the antilock brakes, the safety record and crash reports, and the quietness of the drive when the windows are up.

The classic "boy-racer," on the other hand, clearly likes the sleek sexy line of the Jaguar's body work, the throaty noise of the exhaust when the top's down, the gleaming alloy wheels, the CD system with bass-boost, and the phenomenal acceleration.

In both cases they desire an identical car, but the reason for buying is completely different each time. The same rule must be applied to each of your presentations:

> **Translate your "point" into the professional language used by your audience**.

If you're a geophysicist talking to an audience of accountants don't do the same presentation about rocks and fissures that you would do to an audience of other geophysicists. Talk to accountants in terms of money—translate your "point."

If you're a creative advertising person presenting a touchy-feely ad campaign to a company run by a group of engineers, you know what point you want to get across. But you must talk in factual, definite terms to most engineers. If you don't find a way to firm-up your touchy-feely point you will lose them and will probably fail to get the deal. They speak a different language—translate your point.

As I sit here in a Scandinavian hotel room typing this on my laptop in early 2006, I have just seen a Yahoo news article about the Enron fraud trial; a big financial scandal which has just started to rumble through the American legal system. I notice that the chief prosecutor is adopting precisely the technique described in this part of the book. His point is clear—that he intends to make sure the executives on trial go to jail. However, he has to convince a jury of 12 people who probably know little of corporate accounting and even less about balance sheets and profit and loss accounts. Talking to the jury in terms of movements of funds, large-scale, accounts and cash flow will inevitably leave them confused and mystified. On that basis he may not get the result he wants. So he is translating his presentation for them. The Yahoo article had the following quotation:

> " '*This is a simple case. It is not about accounting. It is about lies and choices,*' prosecutor John Hueston told jurors in his opening statement."

He knows as a professional presenter (which is what court-room lawyers are) that the jury may not know about accounts but they all know about lies. He is speaking a common language—he is translating his point.

If your audience is very mixed so that you cannot define them as "all finance people" or "all geologists" or "all sales" or "all senior management" or "all doctors," then you need to boil it down to the lowest common denominator. If you want to carry the day have something in there that addresses your point in a language they all understand. Just like, "Lies and choices."

One last point ... then I'll move on

You must always bear in mind that corporate audiences are not against you. They are *for* themselves! Your presentation must always talk to them directly. It must alert, alarm, attract, and activate. So under "the Point" you have written at the top of the sheet of paper, now write a note about exactly how you are going to get your point across. By the way, if you're not sure *ask* someone. It is often possible to find out who your audience will be and to identify someone in that group who will be there. I do this type of research a great deal before I present anywhere. I will ask an intending audience member:

1. What do you want to hear about?
2. What don't you want to hear about?
3. What do you need to learn during my presentation to make the time spent listening to me, time well spent?
4. What would send you to sleep?

POINT: "The point of my presentation is to increase the sales of the new product so that I finally earn a promotion to Sales Director"

AUDIENCE: The audience will all be our sales people. They are interested mainly in their short-term or immediate financial gain and want to be convinced how easy it will be to sell the product. There are a few cynics out there so I need to show proof.

Need to announce the new sales competition. Talk about commission.

3. Why that content?

You know, now, that two key reasons that audiences don't remember much of most presentations are that there's too much stuff in them and because the presenters do not bother to learn the language of the audience. So now you know better than to launch into a sea of waffle and stuff.

But there's something else too, and this far into the book I think you're ready for it. A very big chunk of the time spent sitting listening and watching your presentation—the bit between the opening and the close usually—is probably going to be forgotten by the audience, unless you know a little secret. I am going to reveal this secret in the next few pages. As a matter of fact there are several little secrets and I want you to discover most of them yourself right now.

So before you do anything else would you get hold of a watch with a second hand ... got one? ... Good ... yes and another piece of paper and a pen ... OK.

Now I want you look at all the words in the box on page 48 and do your best, over the next 60 seconds, to remember them all. Do not write anything down. Just look at them. Once you have done that for one minute, close the book. Then without opening it again write down on the piece of paper as many words as you can remember. Ready ... Go!

When we carry out this exercise as part of a presentation skills program, the class recognize the problem straightaway and without knowing it discover most of the secrets.

First of all there's the bad news: nobody has remembered everything—a clear demonstration of why too much stuff in your presentation is a recipe for failure. Then the good news: everybody has generally remembered something, quite a few things in fact. However, it is also clear that all the people

box   bottle   plug

dog   kettle   phone

roof   battery   tiger

tree   smooth   book

pen   five   ticket

money   snow   roof

road   hay   gas   chair

foot   candle   flight

cable   mystery   plastic

Jennifer Lopez   mask

cat   roof   case

big   pot   box

pencils   lost

presentation skills   fire

grass   hook   guest

trigger   bag   mirror

paper   roof   stick

have remembered different things. And some words they remember were not there at all ... oh dear.

On the other hand, around 80% of the class have remembered a few of the same things, and these tend to fit a "secret" pattern. A pattern which quivering wrecks can apply to their own presentations to make sure that they are remembered.

Brain retention secret 1: the beginning

The first noticeable part of the pattern is that 80% of people tend to remember three or four words which are at the start of the list. The same applies to almost any assembled audience: they generally remember what happened at the start. So the opening of your presentation needs to have something more than, "Good morning, today I'm going to talk about ..." We will talk about openings in more detail a little later.

Brain retention secret 2: the end

The second noticeable point is that a similar high percentage of people can recall the three or four words at the end of the list. Again, the same thing occurs in almost any assembled audience. The majority of people tend to easily recall what happened at the end of the show or presentation. So, we will also discuss the way to compile powerful endings later in this section.

The diagram on page 50 shows the retention graph for most brains. This applies universally *unless* some "cunning plan" is applied to the middle section. Psychologists call the effect primacy (words from the beginning of the list) and recency (words from the end of the list).

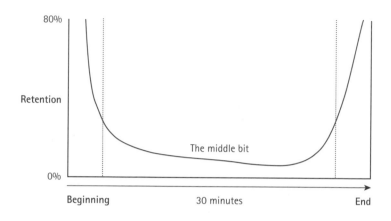

So what about the middle?

Look back at the words you wrote down in the memory test earlier. I would take a bet that, as well as words from the beginning and end of the list, there are almost certainly three other words or groups of words there.

I am going to take a gamble and write them here: "roof" "Jennifer Lopez" "presentation skills." So why do those stick in the memories of most people? And how can you, a quivering wreck, use this revelation, to force your corporate audiences to remember what you want them to remember and for the right reasons? I am about to show you.

Brain retention secret 3: repetition

The first word "roof" is generally remembered because human brains tend to remember things which are repeated. Look through the list and you will see "roof" is there four times. Good presenters repeat the same words and phrases and summarize constantly.

Brain retention secret 4: unusual emphasis

"Jennifer Lopez" stands out like a sore thumb because it is unexpected in such a boring list of everyday words. Human brains love unexpected and unusual things and tend to remember them. Good presenters find unusual and creative ways to emphasize the points they want to make.

Brain retention secret 5: words and phrases directly connected in any way especially with the subject or title

"Presentation skills" is a phrase connected directly with the subject of this book. Human brains tend to focus on words and phrases contained in the title or directly connected with the subject. For example, as well as "presentation skills," "fear," "nerves," and, "voice" would all be remembered for the same reason.

And there is a quick memory bonus here too. Something which the list-exercise at the start of this chapter does not demonstrate.

Brain retention secret 6: tell me a story

The final and extremely important tool you have for your memory arsenal is *the story*.

Human brains love a story. Stories, anecdotes, and real-life examples should be used whenever possible if you want your message to be remembered.

Expanding the secrets of the middle kingdom

The secrets of oratory are important for the success of your presentation so we can usefully spend some time looking at how and why you should incorporate them.

The power of repetition

"How many times do I have to tell you!?" Most parents and their offspring are familiar with that old refrain and the serious answer is "lots of times." Humans learn by repetition. Whether it is learning to play a musical instrument, learning to play tennis, learning poetry or lines for a play, or, in the old-days, children learning their multiplication tables. Top negotiators know that in complex, protracted, negotiations it is a valuable technique to regularly summarize, with all sides, progress so far. Without this repetition of points-agreed-so-far people forget by Friday what they agreed on Monday.

Politicians always try to come up with what they now call "a sound bite" to include in all their speeches, interviews and presentations. It is usually a few words, a motto or a slogan which they endeavor to repeat as many times as they can during a media interview. A few years ago, before my first radio interview, I asked someone with more experience for some advice on how to get the most out of the opportunity. The person I asked told me to make sure that I repeated the name of my company when ever possible when on the air. "When you're asked a question by the interviewer don't say "I think ..." or "In my opinion ..." Instead make sure you say, "Well at <Company name> we think ..." or "The general policy we have at <Company name> is ..." So I did just that, and as a result listeners remembered the name and I'm pleased to say we got loads of phone calls— and many of those calls resulted in some very good business for us.

Professional business persuaders like successful sales executives use repetition a great deal. It is a well known and accurate generalization, that a prospective new customer for a business will have to have been touched by a selling company in some way (letter, phone-call, advertisement, meeting, media interview) *at least six times* before any tangible business can be expected.

Repetition in sales:

The first time the potential customer registers the seller's name but doesn't consciously retain it.

The second time the prospect remembers the name but doesn't understand it.

The third time they remember the name and understand it but don't connect it to a possible need.

The fourth time they remember the name and can connect it with something they might need.

The fifth time they can connect it with something in their business which is irritating and needs fixing.

The sixth time they are ready to discuss using the new company to fix the irritation.

So, in your presentation, copy the professionals—find a phrase or a motto or sound bite and don't be afraid to repeat it!

The power of unusual emphasis

Human brains hate to be bored and love the unexpected. If you want the middle section of your presentation to be remembered, do something unexpected. Do something unusual. Do something unpredictable.

One of the earliest and best-known examples of the power of the unexpected, was the act of Nikita Khruschev, the Russian President, hammering his shoe on his desk at the United Nations in 1962. It was an act that actually had two oratorical tricks built into it and was all the more effective for that. Most adults I discuss this with, even those not around in 1962, know about the UN shoe incident so it certainly achieved its purpose.

Most of those same people are not aware, however, that this message of protest was carefully prepared. Photographs taken during his "presentation" from angles which allow both his feet to be seen behind his podium, show that during the hammering episode, Nikita was still wearing two shoes. He had taken a third shoe with him into the chamber that morning especially for the purpose of "hammering." Harold Macmillan, the British Prime Minister at the time, wittily remarked after seeing Khruschev's shoe-mender act: "Perhaps we could have a translation, I could not quite follow." The fact that this unexpected and unusual action is still remembered over 40 years on, proves the value of unusual emphasis.

More staid and unadventurous politicians sometimes dare to take the "unexpected" step of mounting the podium with what appears to be a full set of notes or even a script for a formal presentation. As they begin to read from the sheets, "Good morning everybody ... [*They pause*] ... I was going to read my prepared presentation to you about educational reform [*the sheets are suddenly and unceremoniously dumped and left on the table. He steps in front of the podium and continues*] ... but I have decided instead to tell you what is really on my mind about our children's future ..." Ah ... this is unexpected ... we're being allowed into the inner chamber now ... we're going to hear what he really thinks. The politician, not a brilliant orator but certainly a good one, has their undivided attention. Good opening too ... but we'll deal with openings separately later in this section.

I was at a kick-off presentation for a management development program in a large multinational company recently. In order to give the whole event some real launch power, the CEO had been invited to deliver the keynote address. The assembled group of 40 managers awaited the new young CEO's presentation with a mixture of cynicism and trepidation. It was less than a week after a rather nasty revelation about some wrong doing in the company. They all expected some politically correct "spin" from this bright and astute young executive. As he began speaking, he invited questions from the audience about anything he said as he went along. [*An unexpected offer in itself*]

After about 10 minutes it was just beginning to sound as if "spin" was all the audience were getting. Suddenly a brave hand shot up in the audience and a question was asked, "So what do you really think about all this mess?" The CEO clearly had a prepared answer for this anticipated question, but he handled it in an unexpected way. He replied, "Well I know what I should tell you … but I feel you deserve to know what I really think. So "Chatham House Rules" … here goes …" And from that moment the whole audience— including me—were riveted to our seats. We appeared to be hearing some major corporate secrets and so we listened. The CEO clearly did not know all the people there and whether they could be trusted with his innermost secret opinions or not. And I don't know whether we were being very cleverly manipulated. But simply the idea that we were all being entrusted with his "inner thoughts" was a very astute move on his part. We listened and remembered everything for the next 30 minutes.

The Chatham House Rule (for those who don't know). When a meeting is held by the Royal Institute for International Affairs under "The Chatham House Rule" the participants may say what they wish without fear of attribution or mention outside. The Chatham House Rule is sometimes used as above when executives and politicians, not party to the RIIA, want to talk freely and confidentially in closed session.

Tell me a story

In the US, "jury persuasion" is studied in depth (there are jury consultants who advise on what sways group decisions), and a few years ago it was discovered that if a lawyer needed to get an important issue firmly implanted in a jury's collective mind, he or she should try to link it with a well-known story. The "younger" the story in terms of the age at which the people on the jury would have probably first heard it, the more effective it was probably going to be. Particularly effective were links to biblical parables, fables, nursery rhymes, and fairy stories.

Stories and storytelling are probably the most common and popular features of all global cultures. We human beings have a deep-seated ability to tell stories, and an equally deep-seated desire to be told stories. For thousands of years, religions have attracted disciples and followers and passed down principles not by factual analysis, but through stories, parables, and tales. Aesop's fables, the epics of Homer, and Shakespeare's plays have all survived for centuries and become part of popular culture because they are extremely good stories. Since the beginning of the last century the sciences of anthropology, sociology, and Jungian psychology have all revealed that storytelling and the love of stories are among the most fundamental traits of human beings. So, as a good presenter if you want to be remembered make sure that the middle of your presentation includes both stories and anecdotes in abundance.

Here are some, quick, real examples I've heard used in the past year as part of three successful speeches:

A large multinational management conference:
"So as we continue to battle in this market we have to remember that a dominant company of our size may not always be popular. It is seen as the feud between David and Goliath. And rarely if ever is anyone ever heard rooting for Goliath ... even a benevolent Goliath."

A technical manager to a board of directors:
"The story of the feeding of the 5000 is well known. 5 loaves and 2 fishes turned into a meal for the multitude. And then the baskets filled with the crumbs that were left. It may sound daft but consider the parallels in the case of the intranet and extranet portals in this company. We don't have loaves or fishes but we do have 5 technicians and 2 websites. These few resources provide a service which communicates to *Fifty thousand* staff and customers around the world. The amount of feedback we are now getting from these people is giving us back ten times more than we had ever envisaged. And so I'm asking you for further investment of one million dollars so that we can perform a similar miracle for the benefit of the whole company in the next..."

A third world health conference:
"But there are two ways of looking at this issue. The way some people want to rush at this now or a more effective way. As Gerry Norris, of the Kings College Institute, and an expert on drug resistance, explained last week ... It's like the tortoise and the hare. The tortoise is equivalent to careful evaluation of the new vaccine, the hare is the immediate deployment of untested vaccines. It appears that the World Health Organization in its honest desire to treat millions of Africans is running like the hare. But we all know who won the race in the end."

A speech to a sales conference (one of my regular stories actually but don't let that put you off)
"Sitting on your chair in your office all day will not bring more business to you. I once had a sales manager whose name was Bruce Cantle. Bruce was a kind man, a successful business executive and also a great actor. He would sometimes appear in the sales office in the middle of the morning. He would look around the office clearly mystified at the presence of so many people, particularly new sales people at their desks who should have been out in the city selling.

Bruce would look around for a moment then approach one of the people at great speed calling the person's name, "Bob … Bob why are you here?" he would call," The luckless individual would start to mumble something about getting organized, preparing sales materials, writing letters, compiling proposals, and all that sort of thing. Bruce would listen for a moment then cry, "No no!! … do you know what that is? … That's a "messing-about speech." You see, you're a young man, just starting out in commerce, and you haven't yet realized there are no customers in the office. But maybe you think there are … shall we look together?"

Bruce would then shade his eyes with his hand as if he was looking out to sea. He would cast about this way and that for a few seconds then say, "No … no there are certainly no customers in here." Then he'd run to the window and shout, "Look, look there they are … down there in the street and in those offices! Quick go out and talk to them, their pockets are clearly bulging with money!"

He would then sweep out of the room to the great amusement of all present (except the hapless yet ruefully smiling, victim) having left an excellent message behind: there are indeed no customers in the office. If you want more business you have to look outside the four walls of your house, office or cubicle."

The above are just four simple examples. You can make your story longer … much longer in some cases. But how ever you use a story it should generally have at least 6 of the following 7 essentials:

- Human interest
- Drama or emotion
- A goal or objective
- Reference to time
- Words to invoke mental images
- Good use of pauses to create a bit of tension
- A message related to your "point"

Some reasons for using a story are

- Creating rapport with an audience you don't know
- Waking them up after lunch
- Preempting a preconceived negative feeling towards your presentation subject
- Silencing likely criticism because the audience don't understand
- Making it easy for senior or knowledgeable people to be told something new without losing face
- Helping cynical listeners imagine supporting or using your product, service or idea
- Helping an audience of prospective customers to understand complex issues.

As Gilbert, of the 19th-century comedy operetta duo Gilbert and Sullivan once had a character sing: "He who'd make his fellow creature wise, should always gild the philosophic pill" *Jack Point, Yeoman of the Guard.*

Good presenters use stories a lot. Do not forget them and make sure you use them.

Go for the chaos theory—compiling a really good presentation

Now that you know what it is an audience is most likely to recall from the heart of your presentation you have to have a think about how you intend to bring together all the stories, facts, unusual emphasis, repetition, openings, and closings. Here is the way most people do this … I do not recommend it, but let us examine it anyway:

Average business presenters seat themselves at a desk with a blank sheet of lined paper in front of them. They tend not to use a word processing package for some reason (more creativity?) Anyway they start to write …

Good morning ladies and gentlemen ... my presentation today is about the problems we face in a global economy and the ways we intend to address them. We, in management, are determined to stop the advance of our competitors. We have spent many hours and sleepless nights over the past few weeks looking at our options and we are dedicated to producing a sound strategic plan. If we look back at the last year we can see clearly that the sales numbers are down on the forecast. The core product line is no longer the growth market it was, and the new products are not yet on line. This gives us a knock-on effect in the ...

[*then they stop and say to themselves ... "No, no that doesn't look right ... needs a stronger opening ... I'll move that middle bit to the start."*]

Then they cross out and mark like this:

'~~Good morning~~ ladies and gentlemen . . .my presentation today is about the problems we face in ~~a global~~ economy and the ways we intend to address them. <u>We, in management, are determined to stop the advance of our competitors.</u> We have spent ~~many hours and~~ <u>sleepless nights over the past few weeks looking</u> at our options and we are dedicated to producing a sound strategic plan. If we look back at the last year we can see clearly that the sales numbers are down on the forecast. The core product line is no longer the growth market it was and the new products are not yet on line. This gives us a knock-on effect in the areas of forecasting accounting and production. Our investors will only give us so much time to address these issues before wanting answers and results.

These days the world is very different place compared to a time when this company was founded by Lord Something of Nowhere. He spent many hours trudging round the factories . . .

[They stop again ... "No ... a better idea would be to open with that" ... more crossing out]

Then they do some more crossing out and marking:

'~~Good morning~~ ladies and gentlemen . ^ . my presentation today is about the problems we face in a global economy and the ways we intend to address them. We, in management, are determined to stop the advance of our competitors. We have spent ~~many hours and~~ sleepless nights over the past few weeks looking at our options and we are dedicated to producing a sound strategic plan. If we look back at the last year we can see clearly that the sales numbers are down on the forecast. The core product line is no longer the growth market it was and the new products are not yet on line. This gives us a knock-on effect in the areas of forecasting accounting and production. Our investors will only give us so much time to address these issues before wanting answers and results.

These days the world is very different place compared to a time when this company was ~~founded by Lord Something of Nowhere. He spent many hours trudging round the factories of the North trying to find his first customers~~ . . .

This process goes on and on a few more times until the page is a bit of a mess to put it mildly. (It's not a surprise that so many of them start to feel the quivering wreck process beginning inside.) They then have a revelation … the best idea would be to start again!

The first page of the pad is ripped off and a fresh white sheet presents itself. The new speech is begun and goes well ... until yet another idea pops into their head ... and another, and another. The crossing out and alteration cycle repeats over and over again. The tearing up and restarts gather pace. The point is that it takes the average corporate presenter at least three or four full days, if not a week, to write a "very average" 30-minute presentation. What a waste of that executive's time. And if it's you ... what a waste of your time.

Even if you DO use Microsoft Word and write your presentation on your computer, this process of endlessly going back to the start and changing it all around, eats up very large amounts of time. Some people just prepare a bunch of bullet-point slides (no notes) and hope that, as each one appears, something "magic" will happen and a persuasive presentation will emerge out of nowhere on the day.

No wonder they are quivering wrecks by the time they stand up to deliver!

Yet in all the preparation chaos described above there is a clue. It is no good trying to force your brain down the narrow constricted lines on the writing pad. Human brains are generally all over the place. Getting a brain to concentrate on one thing to the exclusion of all other for just 30 seconds is very tough. Brains are creative, inventive, almost independent computers, which are always coming up with bright ideas. You only have to inject the average brain with the germ of an idea and it goes off on its own without your help. New solutions connected with the latest ideas. Solutions to an idea you had much earlier sometimes hours, days or weeks ago.

These are usually presented as some form of a "Eureka" thought or mental image. And this normal chaotic process is at the heart of creativity—you can make use of it immediately.

A far better way to compile all the material for your next presentation is by using a so-called "concept map." Concept maps are extremely useful for improving the way you assimilate data, take complex notes and encourage your brain to be more creative. Instead of fighting the chaos between your ears, "concept maps" make use of it. By using a concept map you show the structure of a subject (in this case the presentation of your "point") and the various linkages between issues connected with it, like headings, stories, unusual ways you could tell the story, as well as the raw facts which would be contained in normal speaker notes. A concept map presents information in a way that your mind will find easy to remember and can quickly review. No more constantly "starting-over," because the ideas for the beginning, the middle, and the end are all there in front of you.

Concept maps were made very popular about 30 years ago by an English man named Tony Buzan, who developed part of the idea into a copyrighted system called a Mind Map©. Buzan found that university students could take and remember classroom notes if they did not have to take them down in straight lines. Instead they were better off drawing them in the shape of a two-dimensional structure. The difference between a Mind Map© and a concept map is that the first allows only one central idea whereas a concept map enables you to have more than one. OK, I know I keep on about the importance of a single central point for a good presentation but I know many people will still insist on including two or even three points which MUST be got across in their next presentation. So if you really (really) must have all three, I recommend the concept map instead. A good concept map will allow the drawer to see the "shape" of the subject, the relative importance of different aspects, and the way in which one item relates to another.

You will probably find that using concept maps enables you to shorten the time it takes to write-up notes on any complex subject because they are more compact than conventional linear notes, often taking up just one side of paper. This will help you to make associations easily. If you suddenly think of some important points after you have drawn the main concept map, then you can easily integrate them with little annihilation of everything that has gone before.

Concept maps are particularly useful for

- summarizing information
- consolidating information from different sources
- thinking through complex problems
- presenting information that shows the overall structure of your subject
- making sure the presentation is designed around one point

A concept map is also very quick to review, as it is easy to refresh your thinking just by glancing at it.

A concept map can also be effective as a mnemonic. You could actually use one as a visual aid throughout a presentation to remind the audience of the issues connected to a single point. (There! … as I'm using one to help me write this book that thought just came into my mind.) Remembering the shape and structure of a concept map will often provide the cues necessary to remember the information within it. Concept maps use much more of the brain in the process of organizing and connecting facts than conventional linear notes.

To make notes for a presentation using a concept map, draw it as follows:

1. Write the point of your presentation exactly as you wrote it out earlier, near the center of the page, and draw a circle around it.
2. For the major topic headings (stories, connecting facts

etc.) which will allow you to make your point, write sub-headings, on lines out from this circle. Label these lines with the subheadings.

3. If you have another level of information connected with the subheadings above, draw these too and link them to the subheading lines.

4. For individual facts or ideas, draw lines out from the appropriate heading line and label them.

A simple example of a concept map is shown opposite. It is based around the "point" the presenter wants to get across—in this example—"Getting the audience to understand that St Nicholas is not Father Christmas," combined with a second "point" ... "Getting the audience to understand, as well, that 'Black Peter' is not Father Christmas either." The audience is probably mixed, so the whole presentation has to have a simple, commonly-understood theme—not too theological, but not too childish either.

Once you have all this stuff written down around your central point (or maximum 3 points) you are almost ready to begin. More ideas will come along but don't let that concern you. There is loads of stuff to say in support of your point as you can now clearly see.

To bring all the different items together from your concept map and tell the whole story in support of your point(s) you have to think now exactly how you want to put the whole thing together. The pattern* you should follow can be seen in the following model: "AYEEC."

1. Attention: find something in the map that will get their attention at the opening.

---

* OK, so "AYEEC!" is not a great mneonic but it is far better than the noise you will make if you ignore all this and do your next presentation the usual quivering wrecks way.

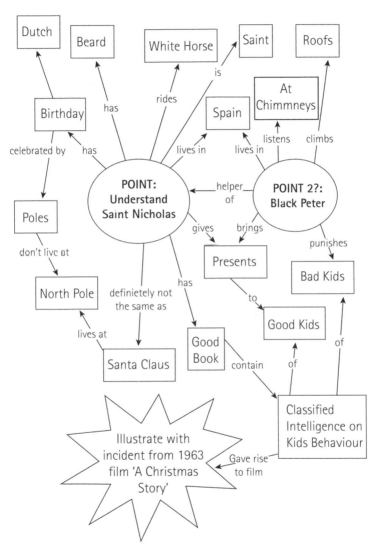

Concept map example

2. You: then talk not about "I" or "we" but about how "YOU" (the audience) are affected.

3. Explain: with pictures [real or imaginary]—even a demonstration—involve the audience if possible.

4. Example: give examples (stories, anecdotes).

5. Close: a big finish is important (leave them singing your best song) when you close.

You will notice, way back around page 48 and then again on page 50 and (again) in the above pattern, that the opening and the close are particularly important. So we need to consider why and what you can do to make yours really punchy.

4. How are you going to close?

I have sat through many presentations since I began my working life. I would say it must be at least 400 or 500 by now. Most of them weren't just awful they were worse than awful. The average presentation ends badly because it appears to be as big a surprise to the presenter as it is to the audience. The presenter—whose presentation throughout the previous 30 minutes has, more often than not, been prompted by the next slide to appear—suddenly hits the button again and nothing happens. A bank screen comes up often sporting a little message from the computer to the presenter along the lines of "that's your last slide buddy." The presenter often laughs nervously and turns to the audience saying, "Oh yes ... well! ... OK ... I guess that's about it then ... so [*here the body language and facial expression becomes very unsure and very quivering wreck*] ... so ... unless anyone has any ... er ... questions? ... No? ...Yes? ...No? ... Is there anything? ... that ... No? ... OK then well [*glances at the senior person in the room for support, in vain*] ... I guess it's time for a break!"

At this point everybody in the audience files out with little clue about what they've just heard but extremely glad, whatever it was, that it is now all over. Even when staying in hotels in countries in which I don't speak the language I often watch convention halls emptying at break times and lunch times. The body language of the delegates in the audience speaks volumes. Generally they look relieved but the shaking heads and the grim smiles seem to say "Whatever we've just heard in there … it wasn't anything to do with me."

Help is on the way

First of all, however totally awful you remain as a presenter,—despite having read this book—there is a little spell I am going to give you. It is a spell that will wake up even the most comatose audience in the world. It is just nine words long and you can only use it once in any presentation. When you utter these words even the dead at the back of the room will start stirring. Games of tic-tac-toe (noughts and crosses) and note passing will be abandoned immediately. People openly doing their laptop emails (this is how a growing number of audience members pass their time these days) will stop and pay attention.

When you say the words of the spell, you will see pens picked up and hear paper rustling as people prepare, all of a sudden, to pay attention. These are the words of the spell:

"Finally, in conclusion, I would like to say this …"

I have tried this out all over the world and it works, without fail, every time. You CAN only use it once in every presentation but it must ring some bell deep in the ancient part of the human brain. As soon as you say these words, the audience understands, at some deep animal level, that they are about to get a précis and some instruction about what they have to do. The fact that most of the time average, quivering wreck presenters fail to capitalize on this knee-jerk reaction is a pity. Academic research shows that prospective customers at the end of even an average sales presentation expect to be asked for an order or some next action, yet most sellers rarely request anything. They say something like, "OK so that's the product ... I'll let you have a think about it ... and wait until I hear from you. Goodbye." And it is precisely the same at the end of stand-up presentations too. The audience is suddenly primed, full of expectation and the presenter asks nothing except maybe a feeble question ... and then ... then ... sends them out for coffee!

Leave them singing your best song

I am not a fan of learning anything off-by-heart but if there was a place for learning and then reciting your set piece message it is here. A good close is probably the most important part of your presentation. It should really set fire to your audience. And a good basic close should have three parts:

- **Summary**: There should be nothing new; it should summarize the main topics supporting your point.
- **Concise structure**: Keep it very much to the point ... this is a précis not a re-run of your whole presentation.
- **Call to action**: It should tell the audience what it is you want them to do next.

"Finally ... in conclusion ... let me say this! You now know why the changes necessary in your company are urgent, overdue and not as costly as many of us once thought. The urgency was demonstrated last year when we discovered that our core business was being profitably skimmed by our key competitors. We know it is overdue because we have seen nearly every other similar business with a 'hope-for-better-times' strategy fail. The tragic story I told you about the once massive Widget Co. is a warning to all of us. And the cost of the change project is, as you have just seen, demonstrably lower than some of the doom-mongers have predicted. It simply requires all of us to apply what we know and do it more effectively. Next week I will be

asking each of you for your realistic forecasts for this new more aggressive approach. Because, without it this company—your company—will not survive. Thank you."

To elevate the good basic close to the next level of professional close you can add a very nice refinement to the above. This is the double whammy close.

The double whammy close

The double whammy is most effective when you have the opportunity to answer questions at the end of your presentation. If you decide that you do want to accept questions make sure that you are:

a) On top of your subject.
b) Fully rehearsed with respect to some of the more difficult questions that might be asked (don't hope they won't be. If somebody asks, what ARE you going to say? More about Q&A later).
c) Ready to be honest and say, "Good question ... I don't know but I'll find out and get back to you."

Why the double whammy? It is quite simple. It leaves the audience with the impression that you were totally in control. It means that the last thing they remember is your key message not the answer to the last question. It leaves a feeling of confidence that, despite everything, including the odd aggressive question, you are resolute and will see it through to the end (whatever it is).

To run a double whammy close:

1. First go through your standard basic close (as outlined above): "Finally, in conclusion let me say this ..." Summary ... concise ... call to action.
2. Then take questions: And not, "Do you have any

questions?" but *"What questions do you have?"* much stronger and more confident.

3. **Repeat your standard basic close exactly as before**: After the Q&A when there are clearly no more questions and without asking for permission say: "Ladies and Gentlemen I would just like to emphasize once again why this is so important ... *Summary ... concise... call for Action."*

To many aspiring good presenters, it all seems like overkill; I can assure that it is not. The double whammy makes sure that whatever else they *may* remember, the last thing they are sure to remember is you and your message. And it is a lot more powerful than, "Well I guess that's it ... I guess it's time for coffee."

A clap trap

I nearly forgot to ask ... how much would you like your presentation to be applauded? Real clapping or drumming on the table or whatever passes for genuine applause where you are? I know you probably work for a company in which in-house presentations, however good, are generally greeted with nods at best and maybe a murmur of approval ... but never "real applause." Would you like me to show you a rhetorical device used by politicians the world over to ensure they get applause at the right point, especially at the end?

OK, I'll show you how to do it. Surprisingly, it has little to do with what you say but a great deal to do with the way that you say it. I often use it, scurrilously, at the end of seminars and workshops on presentation technique. Then, as the applause dies down, tell the class exactly how I made them do it.

The term clap trap derives from 18th-century English theater. Nathaniel Bailey's dictionary of 1721 defines it as follows: *"A Clap Trap, a name given to the rant and rhimes that dramatick poets, to please the actors, let them get off with: as much as to say, a trap to catch a clap, by way of applause from the specta-tors at a play."*

These days a basic method of clap trap technique is fre-quently used at political conferences to make sure people do applaud at the right moment during the party leader's speech. In the simplest example they have a few people at the back of the hall who start off the clapping, on cue, according to a place marked on the script. The rest like sheep, usually join in. But a more sophisticated method, often used by good professional speakers today is called:

The three part list

A three part list designed to generate applause consists of a list of three important points (usually connected to some-thing the other side haven't done or some past problem. This is immediately followed by a single emphatic announcement about the current—excellent—state of affairs now (under our side's control) or what it will be like when our side does get control. An important part of this, as well, is the repeating-rhythm of the sentence construction and the way the presenter's body is used during the delivery of the clap trap. Typically it goes like this: [*Presenter's body kept very still—voice moderate*] "The other side said they would reduce taxes ... but they didn't. [*Pause ... looks around audience—voice still moderate*] ... The other side said they would improve our schools ... but they didn't. [*Pause looks around audience again—voice still moderate*] The other side said they would improve our hospitals ... but they didn't ... But [*Presenter's body starts moving emphatically up and down, leaning forward on every word—voice considerably louder*] **our side is ready and most *definitely* will!**

At this point and just about 100% guaranteed, the whole audience will start to applaud. The thing is, it has more to do with rhythm, body language, and emphasis than anything that is actually said.

It's all in the rhythm:

Blah de blah de blah....blah blah blah [*Still*]

Blah de blah de blah....blah blah blah [*Still*]

Blah de balh de blah....blah blah blah [*Still*]

BLAH ... BLAH ... BLAH ... DE BLAH! ... BLAH! ... BLAH!! [*Movement— emphatic voice tone*]

Think nobody uses this today? You will find it enlightening to watch an experienced presenter, especially a seasoned politician, at the next televised party conference. You will— much to your horror or amusement—see how this three part clap trap technique is used over and over again and applause always follows. If you decide to use it, your various colleagues and enemies will wonder how you did it—now you know.

5. How are you going to open?

A farmer had a donkey. It was a docile family pet. The farmer's kids loved the donkey and it was cuddled, stroked, and caressed constantly. Despite the average donkey's reputation for obstinacy this one was just terrific and would come when called without needing to be beaten or ill-treated in any way. One morning the farmer went out to feed it as normal. But instead of the donkey, trotting across its field toward him, the donkey remained where it was. It just sat! The farmer called the animal and called again but still the donkey didn't move. He crossed the field to where the donkey was sitting and found that it seemed to be in perfectly good health; it just didn't want to budge.

Mystified the farmer called the vet who agreed to come out and see what was wrong. When the vet arrived he and the farmer began to walk across the field toward the donkey. The farmer was telling the vet, on the way, about the animal's "pet" status. How the animal was never harmed in any way, how everybody always spoke kindly to it and, normally, that was enough. The vet agreed that he would also speak kindly to the animal. The farmer was surprised, therefore, as they reached the spot at which the donkey was resting, to see the vet pick up a long straight stick that was lying in the field. As he watched the vet walked up to the sitting donkey and gave it an enormous whack across the head with the stick. The farmer immediately remonstrated with the vet. "I thought you were going to speak quietly to the animal!" he exploded, "Yes, I am going to speak quietly to him," said the vet, "but first I have to attract his attention!"

Ask an advertising company to work on a bill-board or magazine advertising project for your company and you will find one thing dominates the first few weeks: the headline. If you can't get the prospective customer into the top line how are you going to get them to read the rest of the ad? Why do you think newspapers have headlines and why are they always provocative and somewhat dramatic? Words like DRAMA! SHOCK! TERROR! abound even in more serious newspapers. The satirical UK magazine *Private Eye* used to publish an annual book of genuine "eye-catching" headlines from national newspapers. One I recall was "FLU HORROR PERIL: TERROR LOOMS."

Of course the reason they do it is to get you to buy the paper or stay tuned into that TV station. But exactly the same applies to business presentations; how are you going to get the audience interested enough at the start to stay with you for the next 30 minutes? How are you going to wake them up? Provoke them? Make them laugh? Inspire them? Get their attention?

You standing up with the usual corporate "Good morning Ladies and Gentlemen ... today I want to talk about ..." which is exactly the same thing they heard from the previous three speakers, is probably not going to do the trick for you. Most of the audience will be gently nodding off as you begin. I know all the classic books on public speaking quote the mythical old Scottish priest who, on being asked how he made his sermons so riveting replied:

> First I tell 'em what I'm going to tell 'em
> Then I tell 'em it
> Then I tell 'em what I've told 'em.

As it happens, it is quite good advice which will take you to the level of an "average" business presenter. But in reading this book you are being shown the techniques which will move you out of the average quivering wreck mode into the rare well-prepared-good-presenter mode. And to mark you out as someone worth listening too you need to go to the next level.

This audience you are about to present to, need awakening from their slumbers. So what can you do? Now, this is not the time, for a quick look for inspiration from the more off-beat sensational papers like *The National Enquirer* headlines: "BUS SEEN AT BOTTOM OF PACIFIC OCEAN" or "WD40 CURES ARTHRITIS." Nevertheless, there are numerous ways you can get people awake and alert, which is what they need to be at the start of any presentation.

The best way to do it is to break the pattern. Don't do what everyone else has done just because "it's the way we always do it."

The ask opening

Instead of opening with a statement ("Today I'm going to talk about ... blah blah") why don't you ask the audience something? Questions are the greatest attention grabbers in the world. Sales people know that if you want to persuade another person, a single "ask" is worth twenty "tells." Because, when you ask someone a question it's like grabbing hold of their lapels and jerking them toward you. Anyone who has just been asked a question is forced to think about what you want them to think about.

"Good morning everybody ... before I begin there is something I would like to ask you. How much time does the average sales person in this company spend in front of customers on an average day?"

OR

"Ladies and gentlemen I have an immediate and very urgent question for you. How many large-scale exploration deals did this company sign up last year?"

[In both cases pause for a mental count of ten seconds ... it will seem like 10 minutes. Will you have their attention? Most certainly]

The silence opening

Do you remember the teacher at school ... the one you all had the most respect for. Not the teacher who shouted and screamed, but the one whose very presence would make an entire classroom fall silent. The teacher who just walked quietly into the pandemonium of a classroom and stood at their desk until the whole class rapidly quietened and settled into dead silence; not a word spoken. You can do exactly the same as that teacher.

When you are invited out to the front to make your presentation, don't rush. Powerful and authoritative people do not rush. They walk smartly and when they get to the front they pause [*count to ten*] ... and then they smile and look round at the whole room. If somebody in the audience is talking to his or her neighbor or sitting answering a whispered mobile phone call, the presenter waits until the person looks up and apologises [*they always do*] before carrying on. Average presenters could do this but they don't. And by doing it, it sets you apart as a good presenter; someone to be reckoned with. Even if your knees are knocking, the very fact that you are on your feet, with your eye-line higher than theirs, while they are still seated, places you in a far more powerful psychological position in the "flight or fight" stakes. Do you have the whole audience's attention again? Most certainly.

The coming out opening

We all know the "looney on the bus" scenario. Everything's quiet ... your ride to your destination is going nicely then "the looney" gets on board. The one who shouts "Hello everybody" to the whole bus then looks for somebody to unintentionally torment ("I've got a live rock in this box. Most people think rocks are inanimate but I think I saw this one move just now"). The problem with the "looney" is that he is OK provided he goes away and sits down next to someone else. Then you and all the other people on the bus can enjoy the looney. Trouble starts when he sits next to *you* to have a very loud chat. Nightmare!!

But as an upcoming good presenter you can learn something from the looney ... he has the attention of everybody on the bus. In a business presentation, a really great way to use the "looney" approach, is to move away from the invisible "safe" zone at the front of the room. Instead of staying on the platform, where all other presenters have stayed like caged lions and the audience feel that you're "safe," start to move down into the body of the room. It will be as if the lion was suddenly turned loose. Nobody will meet your gaze in case you "pick on them." People will start to show signs of slight discomfort ... they had planned for a quick snooze ... now they might have to do something so they'd better listen. You don't actually have to pick on anyone; the simple fact that you seem to be getting into their comfort zone and "much closer" than usual, is enough to get the adrenaline pumping throughout the room.

At one of my client's conferences in Scandinavia recently I watched a presentation-master use this precise technique. At the start of his presentation he got the whole audience to come forward to the front, away from their nice comfy positions behind their seminar tables. They had to bring their chairs and form an unprotected table-less horseshoe around his flip chart. There was nowhere for any of them to hide. They all paid attention for a full two hours. It was wonderful. Getting closer to your audience and using the whole room as your platform is a great way to grab and keep attention from the start. By the way ... if you decide to use this opening make sure that the sound system, if there is one, will support you being "mobile."

The provocative opening

Saying or showing the audience something they weren't expecting is another good way to get attention.

"Throughout this company we have made over 100 e-learning packages available on-line to our 17,000 worldwide staff. It cost us just under $1 million to set this up two years ago.

[Pause] We paid up front. [Pause] … Last year not a single one of them was accessed by any member of staff." This was a real shock-presentation opening to the board of a real company I worked in a few years ago. We needed to get an increased budget for effective training and coaching, and needed to show that the money spent on a half-baked approach had been wasted. Being quite sure that the board were happily carrying-on in the belief that all was OK on the lower decks, we needed to shake their complacency. Did it work? Combined with the rest of the presentation—stories, unusual emphasis, and repetition—it certainly did.

Make quite sure if you choose to provoke that you are on top of your facts. Many senior managements are kept in the dark over difficult issues and are not keen on surprises. It gets their attention but you had better be right.

The joke opening

Be careful with jokes.

Not everybody can tell a joke and not everyone finds a joke funny. I have seen Hitler jokes delivered in Berlin, and unsurprisingly they fall flat. I have seen jokes which would be funny in London fall flat in New York and vice versa. A joke has far more to do with timing and delivery than the content.

Mrs Thatcher the British Conservative Prime Minister in the 1980s was not renowned for her sense of humor. Her speech writers provided her with an ironic funny-line which she clearly had not understood. Jim Callaghan (in the opposing Labour Party) had compared himself to Moses coming down with the Ten Commandments, in a speech a week before. Thatcher's speech-writers had written the admittedly not very funny line in reply: "All I can say is, keep taking the tablets." On the day, however, Margaret Thatcher read the punch line as: "Or I could say 'Keep taking the pills.'"

She had simply not understood the joke.

If you can tell a joke then check it out and do it. If you can't or you're in doubt leave it out.

What does all this look like in real life?

To demonstrate how all this fits together I have set out below a précised speech which contains all the elements we have discussed so far. It is based on one I delivered to a conference in Interlaken, Switzerland a few years ago. It was a European sales conference and we had to get the salesforce moving again. They were all spending too much time in the office and avoiding the necessary hard work out in the streets with the customers. You will see how the initial point was set down clearly followed by an analysis of the audience.

> Point: I need the salesforce to understand the need to spend more time out of the office, because their lack of activity is preventing me reaching the sales targets.
>
> Audience: 350 members of the UK salesforce and sales managers. Cynical. Mostly bright. A few key people could get a job elsewhere. Most of the audience are capable but lazy. Need to show them how to get what they want by doing what I want. Like most people they don't want inevitable rejection. They must seek it — need an incentive

The presentation

[*OPENING to get ATTENTION*]

"Good morning ladies and gentlemen. I would like to ask you to join me in a brief observation exercise. Can you tell me how many people you can count in this office.

> [*Show slide picture of the crowded, local, sales office. Step down into the audience and look with them back at the screen for a few seconds. Usual audience shouts: "27" "30" "29" "31"*]

The point is there are *so* many people in it. Do you know what time of day this photograph was taken? It was 11am last Tuesday. Do you remember if there was anything strange about last Tuesday? No? ... Nothing??? Yes you are right. There was nothing strange about last Tuesday. Last Tuesday was an average Tuesday in March.

> [*Talking to the YOU in the audience*]

Now ... I know that early spring is not a particularly great time for selling anything. So I completely understand why sales for the month were down. March is a month which often has Easter in it. Also the Christmas and New Year holidays are not so far behind so I'm sure many of you often feel a bit jaded this time of year?

> [*Show slide of gray thundery sky over a city— Microsoft picture library?*]

And your customers are feeling just the same I know. The weather hasn't cheered up yet. It's warmer in the office anyway, yours and theirs. The skies are often a bit gray and overcast so who feels good? Roll on Easter!! Easter is then a good break to really prepare for the big sales push. Mid April comes and we are all really ready. Sometimes this start is a little delayed because Easter school vacation offers a chance to take the kids away for a week or 10 days.

> [*Show slide of bright blue-sky, sunny day over a city—Microsoft picture library?*]

And then suddenly it is May and early summer. And we all know getting appointments with customers in May is tough because whereas people were unwilling to fix up anything with you before Easter—it being gloomy and all that—now the problem is that the potential customers are working on projects of their own which came up in the first four months. Nevertheless they are fixing up appointments for June/early July. So May is an effective month for getting ready for the Summer campaign. And you can tell already where this is going ...

> [*Show slide of boiling hot day, ice cream, sun bathing.*]

There will be an excellent reason for a low sales activity in nearly every season of the year.

> [*Show slide with fall scene*]

Until we finally find ourselves in the pre-Christmas season at the end of October and once that year-end celebration is out of the way we are back at ...

> [*Show slide of gray thundery sky as before*]

... the jaded feeling again.

And I agree ... I still have to go out and see customers too and there is no good time to sell anything. So it is generally nicer to stay in. And most customers, most of the time when we do see them say: "not yet," "no," "need to think," "a few more weeks," "we'll let you know."

[*At each of the above points ("not yet" etc.) show a slide with another "No!" on the screen. In the end the word "no" appears five or six times on the screen*]

All those no's ... another excellent reason to stay indoors. But there is only one problem with "indoors in the office" isn't there? And what is it? Anyone tell me? Yes ... indoors in the office ... at home ... there is one thing missing ... customers ...

[*Show first opening slide again this time overlaid with arrows pointing at the 20 sales people in the picture each arrow labeled "Sales-exec"*]

Look at this picture again ... There are clearly "no" **customers** in the office!

And this gives us a dilemma ...customers say "no" so much so we don't want to see them ... but without going out to see them there is no business.

[*STORY COMING UP*]

I was discussing this universal sales problem with an American sales lady in Chicago recently and I was making the same point again for her. I said, just as I've said to you, "There are no customers in the office" and she replied, "You're sure right there ... just like there are no boyfriends in the apartment!" True enough I thought.

But that got me thinking about my own teenage years when we testosterone-charged boys were desperately trying to find a girl who would sleep with us. (All boys are the same, ladies, it's just the way we are.) None of us had the courage to even venture the question to any likely prospective pal with whom we might sow some wild oats. None, that is, except one in our group. His name was Harry. Harry was a milk deliveryman. Not particularly good-looking ... actually a bit short and he wasn't at all bright. But Harry had a strategy. It was very simple and to us, his fans highly dangerous. He asked every single girl he ever dated to sleep with him. Harry suffered more rejection, broken relationships, and slapped faces because of his "unromantic" strategy. We all laughed at Harry. But one thing shone through. Harry successfully sowed more wild oats than any other lad in the group. Harry knew that enough "no's" were necessary payment for a single valuable "yes." Without the "no's" there could simply be no "yes's."

So based on Harry's strategy here is the new sales strategy for all of you.

> [*Show black background slide with about 10 "no's" randomly placed all over it in large white text*]

Putting up with some **"no's"** which we get when we *do* go out and visit customers ...

> [*Show identical slide as previously with one small yes in bright red in the centre*]

... results in a handful of **"yes's"** from the few successful visits. So, from now, on we will all go out and seek a lot **more** "No's" because the more "no's" we hear the more "yes's" we will inevitably come across in the process.

> [*Show black background slide now covered in about 100 no's in white font with about 10 red font yes's now showing randomly between them*]

From now on your sales managers will not be asking: "Did you close it?" when you return from a call. From now on you will be targeted on your "no" rate. The new daily target rate is: 5 no's for each person on the team!

In order to gather the "no's" you will have to visit and talk to a lot more potential customers. This is no easy target ... You will have to struggle to get a definite "no." Simply because most customers in this country are so damned polite!

[*Show a head and shoulders slide of photo of a beaming, smiling, happy person*]

They will *not* tell you "no." They will tell you they are "thinking about it" ... they "will let you know" ... they will tell you they will "contact you in a couple of weeks." These are all a polite person's ways of saying "no."

You need the real definite "no's" from now on because all the prospect files of the definite "no's" are worth money to you.

[**Show a bullet slide:**
- **"Definite "no" = $5**
- **Advance = $0**
- **Polite person's "no" = $0**
- **Whenever you get one a "yes" = $Normal Commission**

This company will pay you $5 for every final "no" prospect file you hand in to me. That will no longer be your account to worry about. At each sales visit from now on you will go not for just a "yes" close but for either a "definite no" or an "advance." An **advance** will be a definite next action on a fixed day at an agreed time with the potential new client. An advance on its own is worth nothing until it results in a sale.

[*NOTE THE ENDLESS REPETITION OF "NO" THROUGHOUT*]

You may think you're dreaming but "no's" are what we want from you. Definite "no's" not vague "no's."

In this company from now on we want your "no's."
It's only if we don't hear enough about your "no's"
that questions will be asked. Without the "no's" we
now realize you will not get the yes's.

Unfortunately the only place you will find your five
daily no's is out there with the customers.

> [*Show slide of sales office again this time
> completely empty*]

So next time we look across the sales office—whether
in spring, summer, winter, or fall I know it will be
empty. Because ...

Without more **no** in your day you cannot succeed
with existing customers

Without more **no** in your day there can be no new
customers

Without more **no** in your day your bank balance will
suffer

But with "no's" in your day your future in this
company is very, very bright indeed.

> [*Show previous empty office slide superimposed
> with "Go for No!"*]

Go for No!"

> [*NOTE FINAL CALL TO ACTION*]

I also, just for fun, tested the format we've discussed so far on
a bit of Shakespeare. Mark Antony's famous speech seems to
fit the model quite well. Perhaps the Bard should have
written this book.

Friends, Romans, countrymen, lend
me your ears;
I come to bury Caesar, not to praise him.
The evil that men do lives after them;
The good is oft interred with their bones;
So let it be with Caesar. The noble Brutus
Hath told you Caesar was ambitious:
If it were so, it was a grievous fault,
And grievously hath Caesar answer'd it.
Here, under leave of Brutus and the rest —
For Brutus is an honourable man;
So are they all, all honourable men —
Come I to speak in Caesar's funeral.
He was my friend, faithful and just to me:
But Brutus says he was ambitious;
And Brutus is an honourable man.
He hath brought many captives home
to Rome
Whose ransoms did the general coffers fill:
Did this in Caesar seem ambitious?
When that the poor have cried, Caesar
hath wept:
Ambition should be made of sterner stuff:
Yet Brutus says he was ambitious;
And Brutus is an honourable man.
You all did see that on the Lupercal
I thrice presented him a kingly crown,
Which he did thrice refuse: was this
ambition?
Yet Brutus says he was ambitious;
And, sure, he is an honourable man.
I speak not to disprove what Brutus
spoke,
But here I am to speak what I do know.
You all did love him once, not without
cause:
What cause withholds you then, to
mourn for him?
O judgment! thou art fled to brutish beasts,
And men have lost their reason. Bear
with me;
My heart is in the coffin there with Caesar,
And I must pause till it come back to me.

Audience "Thinks"

Good opening—Bit of a *shock* straight off … (We thought you liked him, Mark Antony!) So?

STRONG OPENING
Yes *we in the audience* can *agree* with that.

Too right!! But this all sounds a bit *unusual* … so why are you here?

UNUSUAL EMPHASIS
Yeah we know Brutus is honourable he told us so himself

HE'S TALKING ABOUT US
And OK you're right Caesar was always a loyal friend to me too … that's why we can't work out why you're having a go at him now he's dead!

LITTLE STORIES REMIND US
Very *unusual* where's this going?

So maybe Brutus got that bit about 'ambition' wrong but he was right on everything else.

OK yeah well we've all seen that Caesar was a bit of a softy too. *Ok to summarize so far:* apart from being a great friend and a big softy he could still have been ambitious … couldn't he?

CONSTANT REPETITION
Oh yeah I forgot about that too … there was that King thing as well- and more than once and he was too modest to accept it. "Friend" "Softy" "Modest" … doesn't really sound like an ambitious thug. Third time he's referred to Brutus as "Honourable" too.

Having second thoughts on that now. Wonder if Brutus is really as Honourable as he's said he is.

CALL TO ACTION
He seems to be calling on us to have a rethink. Yeah, on that evidence. I feel a U-turn coming on

SECTION 4

Communication comes not through words and writing alone but by example and body language.

SIR JOHN HARVEY JONES – CHAIRMAN OF ICI

The language of mime—almost

Having got this far you may be saying that all this professional presentation stuff can be left to the actors while you get on with the corporate "executing."

You are sadly wrong. The world's most successful business people today are still the best communicators. Audiences get to see really professional presenters every night on their television screens in news and current affairs programmes and sports presentations. We also see some top business people now appearing on TV presenting their own sudden death business shows. Please remember you do not have to be great at any of this. Good is quite enough because the majority of the rest of business presenters are so bad!

So what can we learn from actors which will help us present as powerfully as they do?

Body language a big part of your 55%

First, as we have discussed already, body language is the most persuasive of all the quivering wreck's controllable behaviors. It will pay huge dividends to consider your posture not simply from the audience's point of view, but because "acting confident" will contribute to your own feeling of confidence.

In the film *Dirty Rotten Scoundrels* one established conman (Michael Caine) in the South of France agrees to train the other (Steve Martin) in the art of acting like a suave, sophisticated, rich, gentleman escort. The body language moves he teaches are at the very core of what is really required.

- Every move is steady and considered
- There is no clumsiness in his actions brought about by haste; powerful and authoritative people have no need to hurry
- The eyeline is kept high
- There is always a smile on his lips
- Whatever style of dress he wears he is always immaculately turned out.

So next time you arrive at a presentation venue take these steps.

1. Make sure your clothes are clean and tidy and not crumpled or stained. If "they" all wear suits and ties, you wear suit a suit and tie. If "they" wear sweaters and jeans, you can too. If you don't know what they wear then put on a suit and tie anyway. You can always dress down but it's tough to dress up in a hurry. Just make sure your clothes and shoes, and you, are well turned out. *Get it all ready the night before.*
2. When you are called on to speak don't rush to the front. Stand, if it is a standup presentation, smile, walk smartly and steadily to the front of the room. Do not run. Do not speak.
3. Do not do as so many quivering wrecks do and begin speaking as soon as you are announced. So many

speakers start their: "Thank you Jim … Good morning ladies and gentlemen…" as they are beginning to stand up, especially in boardroom settings. From now on you're a big shot so keep quiet until I tell you!

4. When you are in position and even if your knees are knocking and your heart is pounding SMILE! *Say nothing.* Look across the room and around the room at as many people as you can. Keep your head up. Make a lot of eye contact. Do that for at least five seconds once you are in position. OK, *now* you can speak.

Things not to do with your hands on the platform.

1. Don't touch your face anywhere between your mouth and your nose … it sends a subliminal message that you may be lying.

2. Don't cross and hold your hands over your crutch in the classic fig-leaf position … the whole audience will look there.

3. Don't cross your hands behind your back in the classic reverse fig leaf … the audience will think you have no hands.

4. Men don't put your hands in your pockets, and most especially, don't jingle your change … the ladies in the audience will and DO notice and will wonder quite what is happening.

5. Do not fold your arms because it creates a subconscious barrier with the audience. Many ladies do this because they fear that some male members of the audience may be "checking-them-out." The folded arm pose is a way to provide some sort of coverup. Unfortunately it only serves to draw more attention.

6. Don't sway. Many presenters rock backward and forward as if they're some demented individual from a secure establishment.

7. The common variation on "swaying" is "the twist" which is usually a defect in female average presenters

who keep their feet glued to one spot but twist their upper body one way and then the other like a small child shyly reciting a poem at kindergarten. This is often accompanied by the early Princess Diana stance—head-down, eyes looking shyly up from under the fringe.

8. Don't indulge in any unconscious itch scratching, nose picking, ear poking, "wedgie" fixing and all that interesting stuff while on the platform because everyone (everyone!) in the audience will notice more than you think.

9. If you can avoid getting stuck behind a podium then avoid it. A podium means that three quarters of your body is hidden and a huge percentage of your perceived impact is derived from your arms, trunk, legs, and feet. The only difficulty in doing this is usually in a large venue where there is a wired in sound system and spotlighting, so check before you decide to move off on your own!

10. Don't constantly click your pen top or any other gadget top you have in your hand. (I do and people tell me it is very annoying. I am trying to break the habit!)

What can you do with your body?

Lots.

1. Keep your arms apart as much as possible with your head up and palms open. In this way you present an "open" image. It projects a feeling of someone who is in control. Your entire body is on view and needs to remain on show as much as possible throughout.

2. Keep your arms and hands at or above waist level or even down by your sides; it feels more uncomfortable than it actually looks from the audience.

3. When you feel a gesture coming on make it a big one. Don't make it a little "flap" of your hand because it will look pathetic and weak. But a big expansive, full-arm movement that stays up above shoulder level for a full three–five seconds. It looks very strong.

4. Make sure they see the palms of your hands a lot. People are, for some unknown reason, attracted to people who show their palms to others.

5. If you want to gesture toward a slide or some other object, make sure that the gesture precedes the words. It isn't: "So on this slide you can see" [*gesture toward slide*] But rather, [*Gesture*] then, "Here on this next slide you can see ..." The first example looks daft from the audience's point of view.

6. When you do have to point or gesture toward an on-screen slide or some other object behind you, (like a white board or flip chart) ... stop talking ... look back to see where you are pointing ... make your gesture ... then face forward toward the audience again keeping your hand and arm in gesture position toward the object. This means you will only be speaking when you are facing the audience. If you look back and start reading off the projected slide with your face and back towards the audience (as most quivering wrecks and average presenters do) you will instantly stop communicating.

7. Do not grip the podium, in fact, try to keep in front of the podium altogether if the setup allows.

8. Know that you can move around the presentation area but stay in one place for at least 30–60 seconds at a time before moving somewhere else. If you keep moving backward and forward you will seem like a caged lion.

9. If you can, mark points on the floor with a bit of masking tape at which you will not be caught by the projector beam. When you move across the presentation area make for those points and stay there for a spell. Nothing detracts from a presenter's credibility more than a blue map of the Atlantic and a lump of Northern Canada across his face.

10. Smile lots and look the audience right in the eyes. If it is a very large room full of people occasionally let your eyes follow a huge letter "M" over the whole mass of them.

For some inexplicable reason everybody in the audience will think you were looking at them for that moment.

11. Remember that even if your knees are knocking and you are in full flight-or-fight anxiety mode, one fact is always working in your favor … The fact that you are on your feet and consequently your eyeline is higher than all of theirs, places you automatically in a stronger psychological position. They feel subconsciously small, you feel subconsciously tall.

12. SMILE lots. Whatever is happening on the platform (collapse of flip chart stand, fire in the data projector, audience not responding, props not functioning, dropping your notes, podium falling over, forgetting where you are in the presentation) SMILE. Do not give any indication that you are dying inside and wish a big hole would open up etc. SMILE. Look happy and in control. SMILE … Pretend … pretend … pretend. Your biggest crime would be to embarrass the audience by looking embarrassed. They are all so glad it is you up there and not them so look happy … SMILE!!! Point made?

Sit up and pay attention!

Talking of the audience … if you can have a "say" in how they're set out in front of you, chose one of these layouts for maximum effect. A good or even excellent presentation can go badly wrong if the layout isn't right. This is especially relevant if the speaker is a stranger to the audience and is too close and therefore makes them feel ill at ease. This may be your aim with an inhouse audience (lazy good for nothings!) but guests may not want you "in their space."

If you are making a speech or presentation at an after-dinner event it may not be possible to get so far away from the relative strangers at the table. However the convivial proceedings that hopefully have taken place before you stand up should have broken down any serious barriers so "space-invasion" should not be so much of a problem.

Relatively small audiences can often be more of an issue compared with a larger one because the presentation becomes more of a conversation than an oration. In these cases it is better to make sure that, if you can, you treat the event as a series of individual conversations. Make eye contact with each person in the room as often as you can for a few seconds at a time. It is not a staring contest so don't make it more than five seconds max. As it is more of an "intimate chat" than anything else, allow your words to sink in, take your time and really slow the pace down.

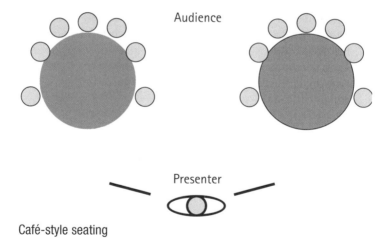

Café-style seating

This is an excellent layout for audiences with four–seven people to a table. This makes for a much more relaxed atmosphere compared with the usual serried ranks of the theater style. It can be a little dangerous as it can give rise to intertable rivalries with the table groups lining up for or against the speaker's point. A strong character at a table can occasionally stir the others up and cause a problem so endeavor to provide a seating plan so that you balance the character mix at each table.

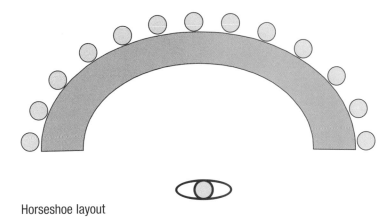

Horseshoe layout

The "horse-shoe" is often used for presentations of up to 35–40 people. In the above example there are only 13 in the audience. But even with a substantially larger group you can increase the feeling of intimacy by grouping the audience "landscape" style even if they are two or three rows deep.

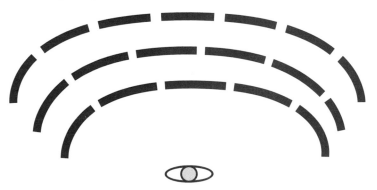

A larger group in the same horse-shoe style remains intimate even when there are two or three rows.

SECTION 5

Other people glean your authority and power from the
way you act and sound rather than from any words you
use.

MARIE TEMPEST – EARLY 20TH CENTURY
DOYENNE OF ENGLISH THEATRE

I'm a big executive not "an actor" ... unfortunately you're wrong

Several years ago the actor Richard Burton held a London theater audience enthralled while he read out names from the London telephone directory. That's all he did ... read out the names. But the manner in which he did it (tragically, tearfully, totally bored, enthusiastically, humorously, with long dramatic pauses and so on) enabled him to control the way the audience reacted.

More recently the rubber-faced British comedian Rowan Atkinson delivered a similar sketch at a charity gala acting as a school master reading out a list of boys names as if he was calling a class register. It was hilarious for the same reason. The names were normal surnames. But alternating between the typical lugubrious, sarcastic, cynical, and threatening styles of a jaded school master, he was able to produce the same effect. It wasn't so much what he said but the way that he said it.

A further serious BBC radio program recently investigated the ways in which the manner of verbal delivery changes the audience perception of what is being said. The main subject of the program was the WWII Prime Minister Sir Winston Churchill and some of his memorable orations. What a lot of people do not realize is that some of the so-called recordings of him in the House of Commons, at a time when there was no recording or broadcast from the Houses of Parliament, are actually the voice of actor Norman Shelley.

But the most interesting thing about the analysis of many of the well-known speeches, whoever recorded them ("Blood Toil Tears and Sweat ... " or " We shall fight them on the beaches ... ") is the way that the manner of delivery (speed, depth of voice, pauses) changes the whole perception. If the words of many of these speeches are read relatively quickly by a person with a higher pitched voice and with no pauses, they have a much less memorable or emotional effect than the one most people are used to.

Research at University College of Los Angeles has uncovered the interesting fact that, when we can only hear a voice and not see the person speaking then over 80% of the person's persuasive power is carried by the changing levels and enthusiasm in the voice. When we can also see the person, voice tone at 38%, comes second to body language at 55% but still much higher than the content itself which rates only 7%.

Psychologists have also discovered that all our brains are hardwired, at a subconscious level, to spot when what we are hearing from another does not "ring true." This mechanism has nothing to do with content but with the manner of delivery. From these subliminal messages, gained from a combination of body language and voice tone, the audience (whether one-on-one or one-to-one thousand) picks up a great deal about the speaker's credibility, honesty, and enthusiasm (or lack of it).

Women in the audience are 10 times more sensitive than men to these unconscious communicators which allow them to accurately and rapidly "read between the lines." Hunches and gut feelings are derived from these same sources. So whenever a speaker stands up to present, an awful lot of minds are being made up during the first five seconds, whether the speaker likes it or not.

Rehearsal and practice are important prior to any presentation. And as "tone" is extremely important to the success of a presentation, critical feedback needs to be requested in this area too. If you can, listen to some recordings of the high-pitched Mrs Thatcher speaking at a normal pace and tone a few years before becoming British Prime Minister in the 1980s. Then compare those recordings with the much deeper, slower, authoritative, and powerful tone adopted later. Somebody in-the-know gave her some feedback and training.

An old corporate boss of mine has a brilliant mind but always sounds dour and very miserable when presenting, and subsequently gives off completely the wrong impression. One of my customers having seen him in action on a convention platform asked me afterward, "Is your boss *really* that intelligent?"

Another of his boardroom colleagues with an almost identical intellect (I only work for the brightest companies!), had a habit of saying, "er" at regular intervals throughout his delivery. The result was that after any presentation colleagues and customers would (cruelly and behind his back) gather in the coffee room and add the number of "ers" they had counted. The content had been entirely forgotten in favor of this sport. He also presented without any discernable passion, regardless of the occasion. During one famous incident, at a motivational sales conference in Miami, he opened the keynote address from a prepared script and in a complete monotone read:

"... are we the winning team ... you bet we are ..."

There are no question marks or exclamation marks or capital letters because, in the manner of his delivery, there were none! He had no idea how badly he came across.

None of us can hear our own voice unless we record it. And most of us hate the sound we hear when we listen to it, not through a few centimeters of skull but out there, hanging "higher pitched" and generally "less classy," in the cold raw air.

But if you dare to be ruthless with your quivering wreck self and record or even better "video" some of your presentations, or rehearsals for presentations, you can (like Mrs Thatcher) spot what you don't like ... then do something about it.

By practicing a few simple techniques it is possible to change your tone of voice in a way that will change other people's perception of you whenever you stand up to speak. The upshot of this practice, if you care to do it, is that you will come across as more persuasive, articulate, authoritative, and powerful.

Constant practice ... feedback ... practice, is precisely what two memorable orators, at diametrically opposed ends of the political spectrum, did during WWII. Both Winston Churchill and Adolf Hitler spent hours recording, listening to, adjusting, and re-recording before they delivered mesmerizing presentations. It didn't just magically "happen."

Major change in a moment

The sound of your voice is a reflection of your mental state and physical health. The only thing more contagious than enthusiasm is lack of it. If you are feeling good both mentally and physically then the way you speak will sound very "up" and enthusiastic. On the other hand, if you have had a bad day, then, if you don't take great care, you will project depression, misery, and a general feeling that "the end of the world is nigh." If your family have a generally pessimistic outlook and you grew up in that atmosphere during your formative years your natural tone as an adult may continue to be "down."

The elements that make up your voice are its musical pitch, its variation in tone, its tempo, its position in your chest, and your own regional dialect. If you alter any single element you will find that the way your voice sounds is dramatically changed. Of all these, changing the tone of your voice is the key for projecting your enthusiasm and generating positive feelings toward you.

So you seriously want to sound like a warm approachable person; here's how

You are not going to get very far as a persuasive presenter and "seller of ideas" without projecting a warm and approachable front. You need to know how to sound like just such a person at a moment's notice, whatever sort of a day you have had so far. Once the curtain goes up on your presentation you have to give the audience a great show. To change the way you sound in a moment do the following:

1. **Anchor word**. Think of a word, which, in your head is linked with the tone of voice you wish to project. Repeat it four times to yourself, out-loud, and make sure you say it with real feeling. It doesn't matter what the word is but it must have meaning for you. My anchor word for a warm and approachable voice is "friendship," Repeat it out-loud slowly and with deep feeling. If you do the exercise as described and the word reflects the feeling inside you, you will discover that your voice starts to become softer.

2. **Visualize**. In your mind's eye focus on a mental picture which brings the key word into sharp relief. What picture does the word "friendship" bring to mind? I see a group of smiling close friends who I've known for 30 years. You will probably have a completely different word and a totally different mental picture. It might be "tender" in which case you might imagine holding a baby's hand

3. **Posture**. Now stand or sit in a way that matches the tone you want to project. The posture of a warm and approachable body is very relaxed. To relax get the mental image clear in your mind, clench every muscle in your body, take a deep breath and hold it while you count to five. Then let it out over 10 seconds and release all that muscle tension at the same time.

4. **Your face**. The actual dimensions and shape of your mouth and the look on your face, will also affect the sound of your voice. One of the simplest methods of sounding warm and approachable is to put on a big smile. One of the earliest things that trainee sales people learn is that you can "hear" a smile on a person's face even if you can't see it. When you smile your voice immediately sounds a great deal warmer. This doesn't come naturally to many people especially those for whom, until now, the world's glass has seemed perpetually half-full. You may, therefore, have to practice in front of a mirror (really) or even keep one on your desk to make sure that you catch yourself happy as often as possible during the day. A friend of mine just last weekend told me that in the month or so since I passed this tip on to him he did (with tongue in cheek) consciously try to smile more even when he didn't feel like it. The result, he grudgingly volunteered, had actually been remarkable on himself, in his family, and among his work colleagues.

Now would you like to sound like a powerful business leader? Here's how

You need to adopt a powerful and authoritative tone when you need your audience to take you seriously and to make sure they know that you mean what you say. You can use it very effectively when you have to stay in control of a situation.

To change the way you sound to one of power and authority do the following:

1. **Anchor word**. The Anchor word I use for power and authority is "firmly." Now repeat the word out loud four times and inject it with feeling and emotion: "firmly," "firmly," "firmly."
2. **Visualize**. While you repeat the word "firmly" find an image that means power and authority to you. I always think of Winston Churchill. The war cabinet are looking at me and waiting while I consider my next move. I feel powerful and totally in control and that makes me feel really confident. You must find your own image … it may be an animal … a lion surveying his domain? Keep whatever image works for you as sharply defined in your mind's eye as you can.
3. **Posture**. How does a powerful and authoritative figure stand, move, sit? Usually they are quite erect, straight backed, head up. How would you stand in front of an audience waiting for your every word. How would your feet feel on the floor. While you imagine this stance repeat the word "firmly" a few more times in order to fix it permanently in your mind.
4. **Your face**. Look in the mirror once again. Narrow your eyes and stare back at yourself steadily. Smile as if you are just about to make a difficult announcement to a waiting meeting. You are the leader … you are in charge and they know it. You cannot be swayed.

More rhetorical tricks

For maximum effect remember your speech isn't just about dumping a load of words on the audience and getting off the stage. Here are three of the most important devices.

- **Pauses** are the most dramatic of all speaker tricks. Churchill loved his pauses. If you have just made an important statement it will pay you to pause … count to three or four in your head … look around the audience … then carry on.
- **Lowering the level of your voice** to make a point, where you might have been expected to raise it.

[*Normal voice level*] "Are we going to accept this *awful* state of affairs for yet another year!?" [*Pause … lower voice*] "No we are **not!** … [*Pause*] "No we are **not!**"

The effect is that the audience has to really concentrate to hear what the speaker is saying as his voice suddenly falls away. Because they have to consciously listen extra hard the words have more impact. Once the effect has been achieved the speaker can resume his normal voice level.

- **Go slow and low for power** is something mentioned earlier in the book. Powerful and authoritative people have no need to rush and are used to being obeyed. One easy way to achieve both these attributes, in an instant, is to press one foot very hard down on the ground while you speak. You will find that your voice drops and slows immediately. Practice it when you're out in your car by pressing your LEFT foot (not your RIGHT for obvious reasons) hard down on to the floor and then read off aloud some of the road signs as you pass them.

SECTION 6

Powerpoint® presentations too often resemble a school play—very loud, very slow, and very simple.

EDWARD TUFTE – PROFESSOR EMERITUS YALE UNIVERSITY

Ah yes ... you probably can't see that at the back

The point was made earlier in this book that most bad-to-average business presenters start their presentation preparation with Microsoft Powerpoint®. Nothing wrong with Microsoft Powerpoint® at all. I'll even go further and say Powerpoint® is brilliant! It is a great, simple, inexpensive, effective, flexible slide-preparation tool.

The problem is ... 90% of business presenters have no clue how to use it.

These are a couple of my typical favorite pointless slide styles:

1. The full-on bullet

THE NEW STRATEGY

- EVERYBODY MUST WORK TOGETHER TOWARD A COMMON GOAL
- THE MANAGING DIRECTOR AND THE BOARD ARE SUPPORTING US
- DEVELOPMENT IS KEY TO THE OVERALL SUCCESS OF THE PLAN
- THE SALESFORCE HAVE AN EXCELLENT NEW COMMISSION PLAN
- THE CUSTOMER SERVICE GROUP HAVE NEW COMPUTER SET-UP
- THIS PROJECT REQUIRES COMMITMENT 24/7 FROM ALL OF US
- THE LATEST FIGURES ARE ENCOURAGING WE MUST DO MORE
- OUR PARTNERS IN PARIS, NEW YORK, AND SEOUL ARE WITH US
- THIS IS THE GREATEST CHANCE WE HAVE HAD FOR A DECADE
- LET US UNLEASH HELL!!!!

The extra little flourish put on these slides used in 95% of quivering wreck presentations is often the build-up of bullets. This is done by sliding each successive bullet into the picture from the top down or side-ways or from top right to bottom left. The background is often very dark when projected on a screen and as the text is in a dark font too (looked great on the back-projection laptop screen) it cannot be seen beyond the 5th row.

2. The senior management quote slide

THE CHAIRMAN'S SPEECH
QUOTE:

".....SO IN THE LIGHT OF CURRENT DAY DEVELOPMENTS LET ME SAY IMMEDIATELY THAT I DO NOT CONSIDER EXISTING CONDITIONS LIGHTLY. INDEED I WILL EVEN GO FURTHER AND STATE QUITE CATEGORICALLY THAT THE THINGS YOU ALREADY KNOW, I AM SURE, ARE THE EXACT DETAILED AND FACTUAL PROOF AS TO THE STATE OF THE CASE. SO IF ANY PART OF WHAT I AM SAYING IS CHALLENGED THEN I AM MORE THAN READY TO MEET THAT CHALLENGE! BECAUSE IF I WAS TO CONVEY TO YOU A SPIRIT OF FALSE OPTIMISM I WOULD BE NEITHER FAIR TO ALL OF YOU NOR TRUE TO MYSELF.

BUT YOU MAY JUSTIFIABLY ASK ME WHETHER WE STILL HAVE A FUTURE TO LOOK FORWARD TO? I WILL ANSWER THAT BY SAYING TO ALL OF YOU, 'OF COURSE WE DO'. AND I WANT ALL OF YOU TO BE PART OF THAT FUTURE"

LORD SOMETHING -- Chairman of the Board

The usual form with this common textual slide is for the presenter to turn toward the slide (back to the audience) and read from it word for word. Little does he know that the audience can read it twice as fast as he can say the words. They reach the end before he's half way there and generally fall asleep waiting for the presenter to catch up.

First of all I have to repeat the point made at the start:

Your slide show is not your presentation ... YOU are your presentation!

If your slide show is, in your mind, a "bullet-point-crutch" to lean on and to prompt and drive your presentation you are dooming yourself to the possibility of terror in your heart and unkind laughter from the audience.

If you must use bullets here are some basic rules:

- Maximum 30 words to a slide
- Boil the text down, then boil it down again
- Use upper and lower case text (all caps make it hard to read)
- Make it bright letters on a dark background
- Make sure beforehand they can all see it at the back of the room
- Don't use too many (or any) transition tricks. It doesn't help.

I once attended a presentation, in the days when slides were 35mm and had to be created by a specialist company. During his presentation, which included a series of excellent picture-slides, the presenter started accidentally pressing the "reverse" button on his remote control rather than the "forward" button.

The man was quite a good presenter and his presentation was in full flow, but he wasn't looking back at the screen so he didn't realize what was happening. The upshot was that his presentation carried on going forward while the slide show moved steadily backward. The point here is the audience didn't notice. Not at all. The main focus, as always, had been on the presenter. Some people in the audience may have thought the literally "offbeat" slides were an odd way to emphasize a point. They certainly fitted the "unusual-emphasis" category, but nobody realized that what was going on was incorrect. They all said it was a good presentation.

But still, to the average-to-bad presenter (or quivering wreck), the completion of their set of bullet-point slides is the most preparation they do before "the day."

The true role of slides and other visual aids is to support and reinforce the point the presenter is making. The visual side of a presentation is very important but that is mostly connected with the pictures, the body language, and facial expression of the presenter, NOT the bullet-point slide show. Proper visual aids are completely different from the rubbish usually seen masquerading as visual aids.

In case you think that underneath all this I'm antislide show let me tell you that I am all for pictures once the presentation has been planned and compiled because:

- Studies at the Wharton Research Center in Pennsylvania show that using pictures to reinforce a presenter's point make a massive difference to memory retention. Good picture slides especially unusual ones make a presentation truly memorable. Whoever wrote that "a picture is worth a thousand words" knew what he or she was talking about.
- The use of pictures doubles your chance of the audience remembering your presentation.
- If you want to achieve your objective of getting your point across then pictures do play a very important part.

But be prepared

One of the commonest Monday morning sights in board-rooms and meeting rooms in cities around the world is the anxious sales presenter getting ready for his big presentation to the buying committee of a prospective customer. The meeting should have started five minutes ago but the customer's data projector won't talk to the sales presenter's laptop complete with slide show. The most senior "techie" in the building is under the table banging his head on the table edge trying to connect different plugs. Then it's discovered that the projector bulb has blown. The buying committee are now outside the door waiting for the meeting to start but there's no way that the projector will work and there's no other room available. So what's the plan? Usually ... 99% of the time ... there isn't one and without the slide show there is no presentation.

First of all, you should always go into a presentation ready to do your stuff even if the data projector—(or if you still have old-technology—overhead projector), breaks down. In short, your presentation should be just as good if you're forced to do it with a flip chart and marker pen, or even on a paper napkin with ballpoint pen in a restaurant.

The *way* you deliver what you have to say, is far more important than all the technology in the world. And data projector technology is still sufficiently mercurial to turn any unprepared presenter into a quivering wreck in an instant.

The most wrong I ever saw a slide-show-centered-presentation go was in Puerto Rico at the end of the 1990s. A large sales conference assembled for a last night gala dinner had, as its special treat, an after-dinner speaker who was a world renowned e-commerce expert. His talk was going to include a Powerpoint® slide show and the large data-projector was set up ready in the middle of the giant banqueting suite. The main meal progressed for 90 minutes or so until it was time for coffee. The room was getting quite warm but the 350 people in the audience were really looking forward to hearing from the international expert. As coffee was served it became apparent that something was wrong. Technicians were gathered around the large floor-mounted projector, it clearly was not working. For the next 20 minutes more and more "techies" arrived and scratched their heads and finally came up with the answer: the warm room heated by 350 humans full of hot food and further warmed by the Caribbean breeze had caused the "overheat circuit" in the projector to "fall-out" (or fall in). Nothing could be done to coax it back on. Once it was "out" it would take 60 minutes to re-set. The presenter was completely lost without his slide show. He had no "Plan B." They couldn't keep the diners hanging around for an hour so they abandoned the speech to the great disappointment of all. Strangely nobody there blamed the technology they blamed the speaker. They all said, "he should have been prepared."

It may seem unfair but that's the way it is.

I was relating all the above to an oil company CEO recently. He listened then started nodding. "That's right," he said, "Whenever I watch my 'Number 2' presenting to potential customers I find the whole thing comes alive and more animated once he gets away from our formal slide show and begins to draw on the flip chart."

Powerpoint® has so much going for it, yet most users stick doggedly to the one thing it should *not* be used for: bullet points and text. But there are six other ways you can spoil your presentation and which, when added to the one we've just discussed these make up the:

Seven deadly sins of visual aids

1. **Bullets and text.** (OK we've just done that one to death)

2. **Rotten Images.**

In these days of cheap digital cameras you really don't have to use stock images from the Internet. Buy or borrow a digital camera (they are really not that expensive now). Take the photo you want and make sure it is one that will enhance your story. Download it into your "my pictures" file. Transfer it on to a Powerpoint slide. If you do use a stock picture (There are loads of free ones on the Microsoft clip-art website) make sure it is not too silly and helps to make the point you're try-ing to get across. Any old picture just won't do.

3. Clip art.

Clip art is fine provided you know how to use it. Just insert-ing a picture of "shaking hands" or a "man climbing a moun-tain" adds zero to the memorability of your presentation.

NO!

But what about taking a picture using a digital camera with the real MD and board members together with people from customer service and some sales execs all pulling hard on a tug of war rope which disappears out of the corner of the shot toward the audience? Make them laugh and they'd remember it. May not be the final answer ... but getting more creative.

4. Crappy lifted pictures.

Take care copying and pasting images from the Internet. The quality of "lifted" stuff is usually dreadful —on purpose— because they don't want them pinched ... especially sample "thumbnail" pictures. When they're blown-up full size they are worse than useless

5. Beware copyright.

Following on from three above, the images are probably copyright and if you use them you could be sued. Hey ... if it's a public presentation who's out there in the audience? You will be surprised to discover how little it costs to license and use some images properly if you just ask the site owner. You will then be sent a high quality image that you can be proud of. One site which has some excellent cartoons from *The New Yorker* magazine will license use of their cartoons for as little as $US75.00 each (2006) and you can also arrange reprints for up to 10,000 hard copies for that one-off price too. (www.cartoonbank.com)

6. Because they're there.

Any old picture won't do. Showing a picture of "head office" just because you happen to be talking about something the MD and board have announced will really not help get your message across to your customer service people (although it might conceivably help establish your credibility with an client audience from a foreign country). Think before you include any image: Is this helping to get my point across?

7. Great, we've got a video

Many quivering wrecks are very pleased to discover a 10-minute, vaguely relevant video that will use up a big chunk of time in their presentation. Trouble is we (the audience) see videos all the time on TV and if it's boring we can change channels. Here in the presentation we have to sit and watch the whole thing whether we like it or not. In my early days as a professional presenter/trainer I found that the video sections were always rated lowest on the final "feedback sheets." As a general rule a business audience is bored with the video after just one minute and something between asleep or completely disconnected after two minutes. So make it a rule that 60 seconds of video is maybe OK and 90 seconds max if you absolutely must. Anything over that and you're dead.

So what does work on the visual front?

Visual aids are much more than just the Powerpoint slide show. As well as adding memorability to a presentation, they can make the audience laugh and add variety to every type of presentation. Don't be too scared of stepping out of your comfort zone a bit. You have your point to get across and you are competing for attention; you must find a way to be unusual if you want to be remembered.

It is very rare that even a "senior management" audience doesn't want the chance to smile. I have just accepted an invitation to speak at a serious conference in a rather volatile city in the Middle East. The subject was very dry and it was with some trepidation that I accepted the assignment. I told the organizers of my concern in an email. The gentleman in charge wrote back a long pleading email that I should not cancel. He wrote (in Upper Case too) "PLEASE, PLEASE DO COME AND DO MAKE US LAUGH AND INVOLVE THE WHOLE AUDIENCE. WE WANT TO PARTICIPATE. WE WANT TO ENJOY YOUR TALK."

Visual aids actually include all types of theatrical props, live demonstrations, packages or envelopes which the audience have to open, and activities they have to take part in. The more you can employ *all* the senses of the audience: sight, smell, taste, touch, and hearing, the more you will brand your message into the combined audience mind. Using imaginative visual aids in a presentation brings any talk, seminar or convention to life, and it also makes sure there is a lot of irresistible humor contained in it. In fact, usually the humor will come from the audience, when they see the prop being used by you (or worn by you), or better still when they see one of their colleagues in the front row wearing, holding or using a great prop.

Let me give you a few examples which I have used very successfully.

A dollar bill

I used Scotch tape to fix a one dollar bill under the seat of each audience member's chair. They were an inactive sales force who needed motivation. At the end they were all asked to stand and look under their chair. As they discovered the bills the final call to action was: "If you want the bucks you have to get off your butts" (Laughter? Yes, and some of them—15 years on—still show me those dollar bills when I meet them).

The chair they're sitting on

Tell them half way through the presentation that there is a white cross chalked under one of the audience chairs. That person is going to have to stand and give a 30-second précis of the whole speech. Of course they are not really going to but it can be used as an example of how we can influence heart rates and anxiety of others by what we do and say. Ask at the end how they feel once they know it's not them ... how does that change the feeling and anxiety?

An imaginary lemon

Asking an audience to each hold an imaginary half lemon in their hand and watch the juice run down their finger for a few seconds is a terrific way to illustrate the way the imagination can be used to influence people in advertising and selling. The watering mouth in the presence of a real lemon softens up even the most skeptical person.

Tin cans

I saw a communications manager once convince his MD to allocate more funds for a backup communications system with a tin can telephone. (Two tin cans connected by a long piece of string) he asked the boss—in the front row—to hold one end of the network (a tin can) while he spoke into the can at the other at the end of the taut string. After 10 seconds talking he cut the string with scissors and asked the MD why he couldn't hear his voice in the tin can any more. The answer was obvious. Now if there had been a second string ...

A real lemon

This a terrific visual and touchy-feely prop which I've used a lot. Depending on the presentation you can give everyone in the audience a lemon to take home. It can be used to reinforce a great many points and themes which you need the audience to take on board. These include stimulating as many senses as possible. A lemon is tactile, it has bright color, sharp smell, humorous associations, sharpness, and it is very simple. A lemon is a great prop when you are training-the-trainer and training people to give presentations. It is also excellent for making a point about impact and making things memorable.

Site safety helmet

For Health and Safety at Work presentations this is still a good aid emphasizing the need to be properly prepared and equipped for the job ... It is still good in the building trade and also for gathering information, compiling facts and evidence. It can also be used for unusual emphasis in situations where you would least expect to see it. Accountancy or computer environments, for example.

A chef's tall hat

I often use it when discussing with groups the need to put a different mix of activities and behaviors into their lives, if they seriously want to change something. As preparation of anything is so often overlooked this is also a great prop. To discuss aspects of mixing, teams, selecting ingredients, identifying and choosing components, people, suppliers, methods. (Be careful with this one. A friend of mine used this prop and kept it on to the end of his presentation. Trouble was he still had it on when he went down to the London Underground station afterwards with his overcoat on. He wondered why every other passenger kept staring at him.)

Set of tools

A mechanical toolkit is always a good one especially when you produce it unexpectedly in a routine business presentation. Hammer, saw, drill ... They may all look different but they are all necessary to complete a job. A good metaphor for group of products, methods, materials, documents, team members etc. Each one designed or trained for a specific purpose, and related to the other items in the set.

A candle on a saucer

I was really stuck recently on how to get a group of disenchanted and cynical executives mentally branded with the need to do something. At breakfast in the Scandinavian hotel I was staying in—candles everywhere—it suddenly struck me. I borrowed a tall candle from the hotel and stuck it on a saucer with a bit of melted wax. At the end of my presentation I told the audience that I would demonstrate the real power of thought by lighting the candle then getting them to simply "imagine" the candle going out. This thought process I told them was very powerful and they would see what could happen simply through the power of thought alone to extinguish the flame.

They all sat there for a silent, tense couple of minutes staring at the flickering flame—was it? ... no ... yes ... no ...

At the end of two minutes I suddenly stepped forward and with wet fingers pinched out the flame and broke the deafening silence: "What a load of rubbish. If you want something to happen in life sitting thinking won't do it. You have to take action."

Then I gave them a candle each to take home. The candles are still on everyone's desks and the manager has even had a reminder "candle" poster printed and displayed in every office.

Bread and butter

Another good one to produce when you need them to stick to the basics instead of rushing off in search of an easy alternative. The answer to life isn't some intergalactic spell but usually the answer to the question: "How well do you do the ordinary things?"

Miner's light lamp headband

A good prop for encouraging sales people to do more prospecting. Any work requiring the audience to seek, look, find, and search. This is very good for cold calling themes and also for researching information

Large Yellow Pages telephone directory or train timetable

When the audience needs to research facts, obtain evidence, know their facts before they set out, obtain detailed product knowledge, understand the detail of a project. Its size (could also be a legal tome) could also be useful as a laughter provoking threat in the event of an omission, breach, mistake or transgression. And there is the old "throw the book at someone" expression.

Any surveying or design equipment

Provided it is large enough to see (set square, tape-measure). To reinforce the need for accuracy and measurement. "That which doesn't get measured doesn't get done."

Builder's level

To make an ethical point and reinforce the need for a level-playing-field, fairness, even-handedness. When you need the audience to understand the need for care in construction of anything or when you need to establish a sound base.

Bricks and rocks

I actually bought a lightweight rubber brick in a joke store once and having knocked it against the podium while kicking (unseen with my foot) convinced them it was real, suddenly threw it into the audience. Great effect. Use it whenever you need to reinforce the need for strength, durability, and reliability.

Large lunar telescope

I borrowed one from a store and had it wheeled on to the platform under a black sheet while I spoke about the absence of information on markets and competitors. I then unveiled it at the point at which the parallel was being drawn between the galaxy and our business. It can be used in a similar way for any presentation on field research, business intelligence and competitor information, annual forecasting, looking ahead, seeking the right answers or visionary leadership. I suppose you could use a domestic pair of binoculars or a plastic telescope but I don't think it would have the same dramatic impact.

Inflatable world

You can get plastic blow-up globes in most novelty and toy shops now. I purchased a large one in the London Science Museum store and had it on stage next to me deflated as I began the conclusion of my presentation to a franchised travel group. As I spoke for the final three minutes I had a helper behind the scene slowly inflate it with a silent electric inflator. It grew and grew as the presentation reached its climax and the audience couldn't take their eyes off it ... or forget it: Great! Any presentation to a travel agency or travel company, any group involved in global markets, audiences seeking international expansion, international partners, the hot topic of globalization sourcing, international transport, import/export, international lawyers, foreign exchange conversion, or foreign exchange rates, time changes between continents, global cultures, ethnicity, Global warming.

Large beach ball

Different colored sections. Ask the audience to your left to write down what colors make up the ball. Ask the audience to your right to write down the colors they see, and then the audience in the middle. If you get the right sort of ball, with different colors all round, you will find they all give different answers. There is only one ball but many different perceptions. There is only one company/community/sales team/ reality etc. but many different views depending on your job, your mindset, and attitude.

Large pickle jar

Tell the audience the jar represents one 24 hour day. In front of the audience, fill the jar up slowly first with very large potatoes, then smaller unshelled peanuts then uncooked kidney beans, then sugar, then finally (if you can) water. At each stage ask the audience if the jar is full yet. At each stage shake the previous load down, then pour in the next batch of progressively smaller sized material. When asked the audience will tell you, at each stage, that "it isn't full yet." Then finally ask them all what they think the demonstration was all about. Someone will always say that it shows if you're properly organized you can always fit more into a day. You should tell them that is not what the demonstration shows. What it does show is that unless you plan to put the most important "big-potato" things into your day first, it will get so full of the small stuff that there will be no room or time for the things that really matter. An excellent way to show how time is used up and frittered away if you don't watch out.

An old fashioned alarm-clock

Get one in a novelty store with the two big bells on top. Wind it up and set it to go off toward the end of your presentation. Use it to make a point about a deadline, wake-up calls or a call to action.

A muscle worker or exercise weights

Bring one on to the platform at the end of your presentation. Make a play of reading the accompanying exercise chart (or make something up) about a muscle-bound toned body in no time at all. Do a couple of exercises then relate the story of the teenager who sent away for the gadget and over a three-week period went through every exercise on the chart. He then sat down and wrote a letter to the gadget company: "Dear company, I have completed your course of exercises ... Please send me the muscles!" Attending the seminar meeting or convention and just listening will not change anything. To make changes action is required.

Nodding bulldog from the back of a car

Set it up on a table as you walk on to the platform. Tell the audience loyalty is all very well but don't be a "Yes man" be somebody who makes a difference. Telling me what you think I want to hear is not what I want. Don't just be a nodding bulldog and in your own team don't surround yourself with "yes men." Use this when you want creativity and progress from a reluctant, obedient group.

Juggling balls

I use these a lot. Promotions companies will package them for your next presentation. Everyone in the audience can have a set of three to take away. Great for proving to a skeptical audience that they can learn in 30 minutes to do something that looks too hard at the outset. Juggling balls are called "THUDS" because you will drop them often during the learning process. You cannot do anything creative without making mistakes. Use them to teach people how to coach each other or become more creative. They are a great metaphor for juggling tasks and priorities and keeping all the balls in the air. When the sober suited presenter suddenly starts juggling in the middle of a business presentation you can be sure you'll be remembered. You can also use them to talk about using the left versus the right hand side of the brain. Also, to discuss techniques for relaxation and stress-prevention, or how to have more fun at work and why practice makes perfect. Idea—use lemons or potatoes from the earlier exercises if the budget won't go to juggling balls for everyone.

I'm putting on my top hat

Aspiration and desire are the most powerful factors that separate the average performers and fellow humans from the high living and successful rest of the world. Hire a top hat and tails outfit from a theatrical costumer and even change behind a modesty screen as your presentation continues ... provided that you rehearse and practice, this can be hilarious. Use it to discuss a strategic decision to go upmarket, go after bigger business, improve quality, aspire to greater higher things, increase performance position with the market leaders rather than the price-cutters; conductor's baton, orchestrate, coordinate, manage, timing, time-management, turn up the volume or tempo, and anything else related to managing resources and timescales. (I once arranged to have a First Class seat from a Virgin Atlantic 747 to be put on the stage when announcing a global incentive plan which included a week's holiday on Richard Branson's Nekker Island. It worked beautifully.)

A large framed picture of a famous masterpiece with a clear message or theme

We once used a series of well known oil paintings to launch a financial information product called The ART. The artistic theme followed through all the promotional and presentational material. In each old-master we superimposed the piece of very modern equipment we were selling. It was a winner ... and proved clearly that a picture tells a thousand words. You should always use diagrams, pictures and images when you need to communicate clearly.

A whisk from the kitchen ... even an electric food mixer

Produce one of these from under the table when you want to talk about mixing and blending resources or people, team-building or shaking things up. If you're daring enough, go to a magic store and ask them to sell you a Dove pan. This is a two compartment pan which enables you to look as if you are pouring all the ingredients for a cake into an aluminum pan (flour, eggs, sugar etc.) then after replacing the lid for a couple of seconds removing it to discover it now contains a delicious edible sponge cake. Easy to do ... I've done it ... great applause!

A wooden spoon

Give everyone in the audience one of these on the way out. Use it in your presentation to talk about the "change and check" process (add, stir, and taste). Tell them while most of the world is seeking the easy "new" solution, the simplest tools are often the best, talk about the KISS approach (Keep It Simple Stupid) and multitasking.

Old-fashioned telephone

Junk stores still have them, or even go to a novelty store and ask if they will sell (better "lend") you an old mock up. Ask who invented the phone (Alexander Graham Bell) discuss the original projected purpose of the phone (to listen to operas and theater at home), and how it became the main communications device around the world. Talk about opportunities not always being obvious at the start. How did products like "Post-it notes" and "Correction fluid' come about? Mistakes and accidents are important. How can we become courageous enough to make sure we have more of them in order to come across the occasional success.

A light bulb

Thomas Edison invented the light bulb (get a novelty one from a magic store that lights up when held in your hand, not connected to any wires). Ask the audience how many attempts Edison had before he perfected the electric bulb. (Over 1000). Talk about the importance of persistence to any successful venture. Remind the audience of what Edison said: "Most people miss opportunity because it's dressed in overalls and looks like work!"

A large steel ladle or a massive silver spoon

There are many uses for these long-handled props. Good for making sure that an audience which may possibly be tempted to indulge in mild corruption or backhanders, one day, take care. Financial compliance, under the table cash payments, you will almost definitely be found out. Quote: "When you sup with the Devil make sure you have a spoon with a long handle." Or use the value side of the precious metal to inspire people, never suggest failure. This can be opposite to the wooden spoon idea which can be a metaphor for last place.

A long cane (a bean pole from a garden center)

Get six to twelve people from the audience on the platform with you. Place the pole on the ground between them. Split the group in half (half on one side and half facing them on the other). Now lift the pole waist high, parallel to the floor between the two halves of the group and ask them all to extend their index fingers and bend their arms at the elbow. Now get them to support the pole between them on the edge of their straight index fingers so that everyone is touching the pole. Once the pole is stable ask them as a team to lower the pole to the floor, each of them maintaining finger contact with the pole. They will find, to their dismay that, provided they all maintain single finger contact with the pole the pole will inexorably rise into the air. Why does this happen? How does this apply to teams sometimes? What happens sometimes in teams who all think they are working toward the same goal? Why do things go in the opposite direction to that intended so often? What can be done about it in our work teams?

A deck of playing cards

These can be used for a variety of purposes. You can get large-sized packs from most magic stores. One of the best and most effective is actually available on-line. To perform it live show a line of six mixed picture cards from red and black suits (Kings, Queens, Jacks). Ask everyone in the audience to think of a card in the display. Take the cards and place them face down in a shallow tray on the table (a box top will do). After a few seconds during which the audience should really try to imagine the card they are thinking of, pick up the cards keeping the backs to the audience and after a moment remove one of the cards. Then display again the faces of the five remaining cards. The audience will be shocked to find that the card they were thinking of (not a word spoken remember) is missing from the line-up. How is this done? Actually it's very simple. (See: www.caveofmagic.com/pickcrd2.htm) It is a prime example of the lack of observation in most people. When you show the audience how it was done they will tell you it's too simple to fool them ... but it HAS just fooled most of them. Why does this happen? Why does this lack of attention to things going on under our noses matter in business? Is there anything we missed in the past that we should have noticed? What might be happening right now? How can we make sure we keep our wits about us from now on? Also use playing cards as a metaphor for keeping your cards close to your chest, to illustrate the need for discretion, for secrecy, shrewdness, and taking calculated risks.

An electric flashlight (torch)

A great and versatile prop. I use a large bright flashlight in a regular presentation about the problems of e-commerce. Why do some websites insist that we must go and find a "plug-in" or install a "flash program" or enable "cookies" before we are allowed in? It is rather like setting up a store in a competitive main street of identical stores. Before the customers can get into your store they first have to take a four-minute walk to a man up the road to get a key (free) that will let them in. [I produce a bunch of old keys] Then before they can look around inside the store and because there is no lighting inside [I have all the lights in the room turned off] the potential customer will have to take another four-minute stroll up the road to another man who will let them have a flashlight (again free). I shine the flashlight around the blacked out room and ask who would hang around in a main street getting all these things when there are other simpler identical stores to get into next door? You can also use a flashlight as a metaphor for lighting the way, leading people, finding the best direction, discovering new opportunities in dark corners, adjusting to strange unknown situations, illuminating facts, shedding light on uncertainty, dispelling rumors and getting rid of misinformation.

A paper plane

There are many websites featuring free paper plane designs. These are really good for making the point that the presentation they have just seen is only a start. It is not the whole program. I have often had the design printed on the back of a conference agenda. At the end of my presentation—which will often be a kick-off for a customer service campaign or product launch—I get them all to make the plane. They all throw their planes on command and the take off is often great. Except that within a few seconds all the little planes are back on the ground. Before we finish therefore, the audience (which has just seen how initial enthusiasm quickly subsides) can see why a plan is required to keep the ball rolling.

A planted heckler

I think this was my *pièce de résistance* when it comes to an attention grabbing presentation idea. You can use it too—it takes a bit of rehearsal but it was a complete show stopper (literally). It has everything—surprise, unusual emphasis, repetition, competition, demoralization, visual impact, and verbal impact, and it was highly memorable. The power of a "plant" is greater than I ever thought in order to ask the tough questions the whole audience wants answered. (It *must* be fully rehearsed though.)

I was working in New York in 1997 and was asked by a company to help them present a new product to the highly competitive financial information services market. The launch venue was the Hilton Hotel during the Securities Industry Association annual show. The company with the product to launch had a history of letting the market down with half-hearted products but this time thought they had a winner. Anticipating the cynical thoughts of the several thousand attendees who regularly turn up at this event we hit on a plan to bend with them rather than fight against them.

We set up a little launch theater on the company's well-placed exhibition stand. In this we could seat about 30 people at a time to show them all the bells and whistles of the new product. We hired a very attractive young actress to conduct the launch demonstration to invited groups throughout the three days.

The back of the theater was open to the rest of the exhibition arena so more lowly, uninvited attendees could also see the launch while standing at the back. The lady was fully rehearsed in the presentation and started out beautifully every time.

About five minutes in, we launched our attack weapon: the planted heckler. This man was another actor dressed in the sharp Wall Street suit just like all the other attendees but nobody knew that; he looked and sounded like them. As the early part of the presentation progressed he would get more and more agitated. He would talk loudly to the people next to him until suddenly and in believably antagonistic and bullying manner he would begin to verbally attack the company and challenge the new product. The presenter lady would look suitably aghast and tried to parry with him as he asked the difficult questions.

Honorable gentlemen in the audience, who thought it was a real verbal battle, would remonstrate with the man and ask him to sit down and shut up. This always developed into him getting up on the stage and asking her for more and more answers—which she was able to give. It always took another eight to twelve minutes for most of the audience to twig that this was a put-up job.

However, at each of the five daily performances more and more attendees who had witnessed the earlier sessions would gather at the back to watch successive audiences get caught themselves. By the morning of the third day the crowd at the door waiting for the next show to begin was massive and the organizers started getting concerned that this legitimate but hugely successful event was attracting attendees away from some of the other exhibition stands.

Needless to say the company involved was very pleased and the message was out that they finally had something worth talking about. So the message to you is this: if you have something to say make sure you use everything you can think of for your presentation to make the event come alive for your audience.

SECTION 7

I hear and I forget. I see and I remember. I do and I understand.

CONFUCIUS

It'll be all right on the night

If you never have time to rehearse your presentations that's quite OK.

Just show up 45 minutes before you're due on and then go into a blind panic because your laptop won't work with the data projector on site. It may then turn out that you were asked to send your slides in advance, copied onto a disk, because you are number three on the list of presenters and there is only one PC and no time to plug in your laptop between presentations.

The best recourse then, is to blame the technical staff at the venue. If I were you I would also blame the event organizers, your laptop, shortage of time, too little prior notice, the terrible company you work for, and the useless audience who won't understand anyway. Quivering wrecks do all these things. And because you are in this wretched state and doing all this last minute panic stuff (despite having read this book) you are still a quivering wreck.

People who were quivering wrecks but are now "good presenters" will have realized by now that **75% of nerves disappear with adequate preparation and rehearsal**.

Just reading this book doesn't do it. The book provides you with a set of tools, but if you care not to use them that is OK with me.

The failure to rehearse, through lack of time and inadequate notice, is only a fair excuse for about 5% of all presentations. Even then, my experience tells me that the 5% is really about 3% or less.

Most of the time business people just don't bother ... they hope the awful looming presentation day will just go away ... then, as always, the day just arrives all of a sudden, out of the blue.

The rules for rehearsal are very simple. Once you have compiled and gathered all your material make up your mind what sort of notes or script you are going to use.

Script vs notes?

Unless you have a very formal presentation to deliver in which every word must be correct and checked by "Legal" (e.g. Public Company AGMs) you should not use a full word-for-word script.

Unless you are a "natural," reading from a script always sounds wooden and totally flat.

Voices tend to start loud at the opening
of each sentence then collapse towards the end!

To avoid this saw-tooth effect you definitely need to practice in front of a video camera several times in order to see what it looks and sounds like, whether you like what you see or not. The correct way to set out a word-for-word script on a sheet of A4 paper is as follows:

- Number every page "large" in the bottom right hand corner.
- Use upper and lowercase letters as normal. All UPPER CASE is not as easy to read.
- Use a font that makes the words stand out clearly. Arial in 18 point and black print is normally seeable if you're on stage with lights shining in your eyes.
- Use the upper two-thirds of the sheet only and type only half way across the sheet (this stops your eye then your head constantly dropping down too far as you read each sheet). It also means you have plenty of room to hand-write last minute changes.
- Space the lines of text well apart and finish an idea on a page even if it only takes up a few lines.
- Mark slide changes clearly with a large colored "blob." Don't do a small one: you need to be able to see it clearly "up there."
- Highlight cues for "props" in a bright color: blue, red or green (not yellow: too difficult to see!) and mark in brackets "[Show the walking stick]" or whatever it is.
- Don't use commas. Instead use a row of "dots" where a comma would normally go. This again is much easier to see and makes more sense when you're tense up there.
- If you want to "pause for effect" at various points mark the words "**[PAUSE 1.......2......3]**" in brackets as shown to signify that you should stop and pause for the slow mental count indicated.
- <u>Underline</u> and **bold** every important point in the script. Where you need to lower the level of your voice reduce the 18 point font to 16 point, underline the section and end with an exclamation mark.
- Always finish a sentence on a page ... never carry it over to the next page.
- Have a spare script in your pocket in case you drop/mislay the one you have.
- If you have a friend/colleague in the front row give him/her a script copy too.

- Staple all the pages of the script firmly in the top left-hand corner.
- I also add a little note throughout the script: [SMILE!] just in case I forget to!

A scripted speech should be set out as follows:

The quality of mercy is
not strain'd. It droppeth
as the gentle rain from
heaven.... it is twice bless'd
upon the place beneath.
It blesseth him that gives
and him that takes.

It is mightiest in the
mightiest.
It becomes the
throned monarch mightier
than his crown.
His sceptre shows the force
of temporal power.

1

The attribute to awe and
majesty,
Wherein doth sit the
dread and fear of kings...
But mercy is above this
sceptred sway...
It is enthroned in the
hearts of kings!

It is an attribute to God
himself...and earthly power
doth then show likest God's ...
when mercy
seasons justice.

2

Therefore, Jew, ...
Though justice be thy
plea, consider this,...
That, in the course of
justice, none of us should
see salvation...
we do pray for mercy!
And that same prayer doth
teach us all to render
the deeds of mercy.

3

I have spoke thus much
To mitigate the justice of
thy plea..... which if thou
follow.... this strict court
of Venice Must needs give
sentence 'gainst the
merchant there!

END

4

Note cards

By far the best way to keep your presentation notes together is on a series of plain file cards. The same annotations for slide changes and other changes-in-emphasis as used for a full script should be used here too. This time use bullet notes to remind you what you want to say, NOT full text.

The added steps for note cards are these:

- Use cards which are a little larger all round than standard postcards … most stationers sell them in packs of 100.
- Use these cards in "portrait" orientation because you can hold them better in your hand.
- Number the cards in the bottom right hand corner.
- Punch a hole in the top left hand corner of each card and thread a "lace and tag" (again you can get these in most stationers) through the holes to hold them all together.
- Use only bullet words not whole paragraphs.
- Type the notes in 18 and 16 point if you can because it is easier to read. If you hand write the words, print them clearly using upper and lower case in the normal way.

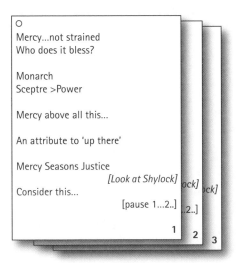

Rehearsal rules

These are very simple:

1. Good presenters rehearse their presentations at least *three times*.
2. They always rehearse them *out loud* not just in their mind.
3. They always rehearse with *all their slides and props*.
4. They almost always *video* their rehearsals.
5. They always seek a colleague to watch and give *critical feedback*.
6. They always endeavor to rehearse once at the *final location*.
7. They check from the *back of the room* that their slides and props can be clearly seen.
8. They try to rehearse at the final destination the *day before* when there's still time.
9. They always arrive at the venue *before everyone else* and in good time to make sure everything is working especially when using their *own equipment with somebody else's*.
10. *They know that rehearsals remove 75% of quivering wreck nerves.*

And finally: "Q & A"

If you take questions at the conclusion of your speech stick to these guidelines:

- Answer questions truthfully and smile however tough the question.
- If you don't know the answer say: "I don't know the answer to that. I will find out and get back to you" (then DO get back to them).

- However tough the question smile and say, "That's an excellent question."
- If somebody wants to keep coming back on a question, raise your hand and (if you can) walk toward them nodding. Say, "Yes that is a very good point. Unfortunately I don't have time to go into that much depth today. Would it be OK if we take that separately? [don't pause, still nod and smile] ... thanks. Look away across the audience and say, "I have time for just one more point?" pause ... If there isn't one ... do your close again and end it.
- Never argue with an audience member; they are your customers and customers are always right.

SECTION 8

If you want experience dealing with difficult people ... have kids.

BO BENNETT

Dealing with the "Clinically Difficult"

Occasionally in your presentations, especially internal presentations where many people in the audience "know" you, there will someone who regards you as legitimate "sport"— a victim to be played with like a gladiator at the Collesium in Rome. In particular, if the "big boss" or someone politically influential is in the room they will endeavor to score points by asking a tough question. This is quite OK and fully manageable.

First, make sure that you remember that a) bullies are generally cowards and b) 99% of the human race loathes and fears public exposure (that's why public speaking is the number one executive fear).

If you have a tough subject to talk about, and you know there is bound to be some negative feeling which might result in a "surprise" tough question or two at the end, you can deal with it by opening your presentation with that very point.

"Ladies and gentlemen. In the past year we have not produced the range of products envisaged 12 months ago. The

anticipated demand has failed to transpire, and you have not had the increase in commission you reasonably expected. So you can justifiably ask why on earth should you stay with this company? The answer is simple: the next six months are going to be brilliant. During the next 20 minutes I am going to show you why your decision to stay with us is going to change your life more than you ever imagined."

More than once, I've watched out of the corner of my eye, as I opened with this type of approach and my anticipated adversary's face "dropped a mile." Your target still might raise something at the end but it certainly won't have the impact it would have done if the issue is avoided altogether.

So a bit of careful advance planning can defuse an otherwise tough situation. In particular, it is essential, whatever you have to present, that you anticipate all the questions you might get—even the nasty ones and don't hope nobody will ask… Anticipate that the "Clinically Difficult" person will ask it. Prepare for your Q&A—as fully as you can!

On the other hand, don't make the opposite mistake which the news company I worked for, Reuters, did when it presented its first annual results after flotation on the London Stock Market. Their Investor Relations department religiously prepared a highly detailed internal Q&A for the MD to use during his presentation. Then somebody accidentally made 300 copies which were included in the press packs handed out to every journalist and shareholder in the audience. It meant they all received a list of highly revealing questions they hadn't even thought of asking. Not a good move.

When you do get to the point when that persistent and difficult person might ask a question, remember one important thing. The very fact that you are "the speaker" and are usually "on your feet" places you in a psychologically powerful position compared with the audience. For now you're in charge … you're "The Daddy."

So as the person temporarily in charge, you have to control your audience. And one of the best ways to deal with a clinically difficult person is simply to avoid acknowledging that he or she has raised their hand.

A couple of years ago I attended a presentation where the speaker handled the Q&A badly. Many times during the presentation, "Mr Difficult" put up his hand to ask the presenter a question. Every single time the presenter acknowledged him, he asked a tough or irrelevant question. Many times he was just "grandstanding" and not asking a question at all. The audience was clearly getting embarrassed when he was talking, and the speaker was clearly getting very uneasy, but he continued to answer him and waffle though muddled replies to his questions.

He had completely relinquished control to the audience member without good reason. The presenter should not have continued acknowledging him after his first inappropriate question. Believe me, there is nothing in the presenter's "rule book" that says you have to acknowledge everyone with their hand up. You have to control who you acknowledge and you must not surrender that control to anyone else.

As a presenter you have many options for controlling a difficult audience member.

Ignore them

You can simply elect not to acknowledge the clinically difficult person. (This is known as the "Cat-String Theory." When you're teasing a cat by jerking a piece of string in front of its nose it will continue to grab at the string. As soon as you let the string fall to the floor and turn away the cat immediately loses interest.)

Set your limits

You can say at the start, "In the interests of time and to ensure that you all have at least one opportunity to ask me something, I'd be grateful if you would limit questions to one each please—thanks."

Ask them to write their questions

You can say, "I'm sure some of you have a lot of questions, but we won't have time to answer them all. Could you please write down your questions, perhaps on the back of your business card? I will get someone to collect them all ... thanks. I am going to answer as many of them as I can at the end provided we have time."

Off line it

You can say: "Yes James ..." [always say Yes] OR "Could I have your name, Sir? James Brown? Well, James, you have some very good questions but we have limited time today to cover everything, would you mind giving me the rest of your comments later ... thanks." Or, "John, that is an excellent point and I want to give you the right answer. Could we take this off-line afterwards? ... thanks." While you're asking him if it's OK, nod your head up and down. It will encourage him to nod in agreement with you.

Politician it

You can also take a line from our political masters. Politicians know exactly what they do and do not want to talk about. And whenever they're asked a question by a "difficult" voter or journalist at a public gathering they stick to their guns and answer the question like this:

> "Yes Sir … you are asking a very good question about healthcare funding … thank you for that. And this itself begs the larger question about funding pensions, and social security as well. Added together, in the past year, spending on all these and other allied programs has increased in line with the targets we announced over two years ago and by double the amount anticipated by the opposition party."

In other words, whilst appearing to answer the difficult question they have neatly side-stepped it and answered the question that they are more comfortable with.

Be cruel

And finally, as I said at the start of this section, cowardice and fear rule in most heckler's minds. They are so glad it's you up there on the platform and not them. Always remember then, that a great way to quieten them down is to "expose" them with a big verbal spotlight. When you see a hand going up repeatedly say, "Yes Sir … at the back … I'm sorry could you first tell us your full name" (repeat it back to them) "And which company (or department) do you work for?" (repeat it back to them) "And your question is?" (paraphrase it back to them).

All this hullabaloo is not the quick "in and out" the average clinically difficult person is comfortable with. If they try it again say, "Yes Mr James Brown again at the back…" You will very often find they don't give you any more trouble.

You must not let one audience member spoil it for everyone else. I am not telling you to handle him in a rude way, but you must bear in mind that the rest of the audience will recognize the difficult person is being difficult, and will have more respect for you if you deal with the situation firmly and effectively. Most audiences don't want to listen to the difficult one, either.

About the Author

Bob Etherington has been developing his reputation for sales success since the 1970s, in a career that has spanned many global markets.

Having begun his career in 1970 with Rank Xerox in London, he was quickly headhunted by Grand Metropolitan Hotels and then became a Money Broker in the City. He joined Reuters, the international news and financial information leader in the 1980s, and became a main Board Director for Transaction Services in 1990, moving to New York in 1994 to take control of their major accounts strategy for US banks. Reuters' international sales to these banks grew rapidly and, as a result, Bob was appointed to organise professional sales training for the entire company.

In 2000, Bob left Reuters and became co-founder of SpokenWord Ltd., the UK-based sales training company. He resigned as Managing Director of SpokenWord Ltd. in 2008.

Bob now lives between his homes in London and Kent and is currently working on a variety of business, theatre and charity projects. He can be contacted at robertetherington@yahoo.co.uk or via the website www.bobetheringtongroup.com.